" *Life is*

PAINFUL, NASTY & SHORT . . .

IN MY CASE IT HAS ONLY

BEEN PAINFUL & NASTY."

"LIFE IS

PAINFUL, NASTY & SHORT

...IN MY CASE IT HAS ONLY

BEEN PAINFUL & NASTY."

Djuna Barnes
1978-1981

AN INFORMAL MEMOIR BY
HANK O'NEAL

PARAGON HOUSE · NEW YORK

First Edition, 1990

Published in the United States by

Paragon House
90 Fifth Avenue
New York, NY 10011

Copyright © 1990 by HANK O'NEAL

Designed by Kathy Kikkert

Library of Congress Cataloging-in-Publication Data
O'Neal, Hank.
    "Life is painful, nasty, and short—in my case it has only been painful and nasty" : Djuna Barnes, 1978–1981 : an informal memoir / by Hank O'Neal.
        p.   cm.
    ISBN 1-55778-394-2
    1. Barnes, Djuna—Biography—Last years and death.
2. O'Neal, Hank—Friends and associates.   3. Novelists, American—20th century—
    Biography.   I. Title.
    PS3503.A614Z8   1990
    818'.5209—dc20
    [B]   90-32196
                                                      CIP
Manufactured in the United States of America
10 9 8 7 6 5 4 3 2 1

To: SMS

ACKNOWLEDGMENTS

*M*any people have been very helpful in making this memoir possible. They gave of their time, offered advice, and were always encouraging. Ben Raeburn edited the original manuscript not once but twice. His suggestions and editorial skill were of great assistance. Ron Kurtz provided original negatives for Berenice Abbott's portraits of Djuna Barnes, most of which have never been previously published. Berenice Abbott herself was generous with her time in talking about portions of the manuscript. Allen Ginsberg led me to Paragon; it was his suggestion that I contact Juanita Lieberman, who in turn led me to Ken Stuart and finally, Don Kennison, who has seen the book through the myriad stages of production. And Shelley Shier, who aided me over the last seven years as this book took shape, gets the last acknowledgment, but surely the one most deeply felt.

PREFACE

Djuna Barnes was born June 12, 1892, on Storm King Mountain at Cornwall-On-Hudson, New York. Her ashes were scattered on the mountain shortly after she died in her Greenwich Village apartment on June 17, 1982. She received no formal education as a child or young woman; her only tutoring was from parents and relatives. Despite this lack of formal education, or perhaps because of it, she began writing and drawing as a teenager and was a published author before she was twenty. She was a remarkable woman in many ways and in the course of her ninety years established three reputations: one literary, one social, and one sexual.

My original hope was that any introductory comments might have been made by one of Barnes's contemporaries, but this proved impractical for any number of reasons, the two primary being that virtually everyone who was ever close to Barnes and aware of her life and work was dead and that while no one seriously disputed her extraordinary talent, Barnes was not universally admired on a personal level. To illustrate the problem one need only take note of Andrew Field's thoroughly researched biography, *Djuna*. The index in this book lists nearly four hundred personalities, but fewer than fifty ever possessed the combined requisites of both being close to Barnes and having sufficient literary capability to write an introduction. Of those with the qualifications only six are still alive at the time of this writing: Berenice Abbott, Samuel Beckett, Kay Boyle, Kenneth Burke, Malcolm Cowley, and Charles Henri Ford.

It is easy to reduce the six to four; Beckett met Barnes late and while very generous to her in the 1950s hadn't really known her since the 1930s. Boyle was never close to Barnes even though they shared a romantic interest in Lawrence Vail, whom Boyle later married, not a particularly good common bond for impartial commentary.

It is equally easy to remove Burke and Ford as candidates. Burke first met Barnes in the teens but had only limited contact with her in the ensuing years. Additionally, the two had quarreled ferociously after Burke wrote an uncomplimentary article about *Nightwood* in 1966, and the two were totally estranged from that point on. Ford was equally unacceptable. He had been closest to Barnes

in the 1930s, but except for letters was rarely in touch with her
except during the period when he published the periodical, *View*.
An added difficulty was that Barnes held Ford's work in very low
regard. That he certainly knew her opinion would further hinder
impartial commentary.

Berenice Abbott and Malcolm Cowley became the only acceptable candidates; both had known her since 1918 and had been in
touch with her over the years. The possibility of an introduction
was discussed with both: In July 1987 Abbott stated firmly,
"Djuna bores me to death and she was a literary snob as well. I have
no interest in writing about her." A month earlier Cowley wrote,
"Owing to the fragilities of age, I have been forced to stop writing.
If I started again an introduction to a book about Djuna is one of
the subjects I should least willingly undertake." With the list of
contemporaries exhausted—and because of my own prejudice
against an introduction by anyone who did not know Barnes
personally—I found the task forced on me. Many aspects of my
nearly three years of activity with this legendary literary figure
need little explanation, but my observations were written with a
moderately informed reader in mind. Some historical perspective,
therefore, may be helpful to those who know nothing of Barnes.

In the late teens, throughout the 1920s, and into the 1930s she
was a beautiful and dashing figure. Extremely attractive, elegant,
witty, and domineering, she was, in many ways, an ultimate
reflection of the times: a woman who shunned almost all conventional values, lived her life to the fullest in a fashion she chose, and
not only got away with it but was rewarded for her actions. Barnes
was equally attracted to both sexes, enjoyed the pleasures afforded
by men and women, and established lengthy relationships with
more than a handful of individuals. Her intellectual friends and
associates were equally diverse and, even more importantly, so was

her literary career as a successful novelist, playwright, poet, critic, and newspaper reporter.

In the twenty-five years between 1911, when her first poem was published in *Harper's Weekly*, until the publication of her novel, *Nightwood*, in 1936, she released a massive amount of work. Forty-three poems and thirty-six short stories were published in various newspapers and periodicals, plus additional prose and poetry appeared in three collections of her own: *The Book of Repulsive Women* (1915); *A Book* (1923); and *A Night Among the Horses* (1929). Her first novel, *Ryder*, appeared in 1928 in New York, and in the same year the mildly scandalous *Ladies Almanack* appeared in Paris. She also wrote a dozen published plays between 1916 and 1923, several of which were performed at the Provincetown Playhouse, often on double bills with works by Eugene O'Neill. Add to these accomplishments at least 175 articles for newspapers and periodicals, many of which she illustrated herself (her pen and ink drawings were regularly exhibited at the time), and it is easy to recognize an exceptional career.

In many ways Barnes's literary career peaked with the publication in England of *Nightwood* in 1936. The book, aided by an introduction by T. S. Eliot, appeared in the United States the following year. Today the novel is regarded as a masterpiece in many quarters and at least a minor masterpiece by even the most timid critic, but in the 1930s it made no particular impression on the public, nor did it generate any significant critical acclaim. At the time it was just another book.

In 1937, Barnes was forty-five; she had lived half her life and was, presumably, at the peak of her literary powers. Yet after the publication of *Nightwood*, during the second half of her life, she released but five new works for publication: a short article (1941); one story (1942); a very complex play, *The Antiphon* (1958); and two poems (1969, 1971). The last forty plus years of her life were spent in self-imposed seclusion, surrounded by a clutter of incomplete poems and manuscripts in a tiny, one-room apartment in New York's Greenwich Village. She had returned from Europe to the scene of her earliest triumphs but seems to have had little or no interest in ever having any others. Her self-imposed social and literary exile puzzled almost everyone.

It may not have been Barnes's intent to withdraw from public view when she returned to the United States in 1939, but the reality is that she did. Her activities from that point on became shrouded in mystery. The literary creations she had fashioned in the first half of her life were a matter of record, available to any reader who might have an interest; much of her private life was equally well-known during her socially active years. She was not a retiring figure but one very much in the public eye. All her writing, fiction and non-fiction alike, chronicled her activity. The only aspect of her life not accessible to a casual reader involved her affairs with men. Barnes was in no way circumspect about her interest in women, but men were another matter, and few knew of her early marriage or liaisons with heterosexual men.

The less she appeared in public, and the many years between publications, only made the mystery of Barnes deepen. As years passed the legend grew, and more literary critics and others with specific causes began to take increased notice of her. Yet, the more the critics and literary figures wrote and the more various groups or publications pleaded for a comment from her, the more resolute she became in ignoring everyone. She never afforded a serious interview to any publication during her years of seclusion, though she did speak briefly with a reporter from the *New York Times* in 1971. She was a very private person and on more than one occasion called the police to remove weeping women from her doorstep.

She remained stubborn to the end. Three books published about her in the mid-1970s were done without her assistance. And by the time of her death, almost every word she had ever deemed fit to publish was in print somewhere in the world, and a small cottage industry had developed collecting and publishing the words she did not want to ever see the light of day. Early stories, newspaper interviews, and even the rejected plays found their way into print.

Djuna Barnes was an extraordinary woman: a literary figure of significance, a skilled graphic artist and painter, a vibrant personality. Much of her work is very important in the development of fiction in the English language, but the two phases of her life and how she lived them, while not nearly as important, are perhaps more interesting. The peculiarity of the second half of her life, particularly the final years, is without parallel in the history of American literature and tends to overshadow some of her other achievements.

In mid-1978, I found myself in the midst of Djuna Barnes's mysterious and reclusive world. The brief memoir that follows is a simple record of the nearly three years during which I befriended her and tried to bring some organization into her life and affairs. It presents a modest portrait of what she had become, how she viewed herself and others, and her opinion of writing. I hope it casts some much needed light on the mystery she had purposely created.

Hank O'Neal
New York, 1988

Djuna Barnes, New York City 1972

On a Sunday afternoon in June 1982, I was on working holiday in Maine with Berenice Abbott. We were organizing a few last minute details concerning our book, *Berenice Abbott—American Photographer*. The telephone rang: Berenice answered, spoke to someone for a few moments, hung up the telephone, and said simply, "Djuna died on Friday." That was all. I don't remember replying, but as I recall that moment I find it amazing that neither of us had anything to say to the other.

Berenice Abbott had known Djuna Barnes longer than anyone then alive except for some of Barnes's elderly relatives. Concern for her old friend had been the reason for her introducing me to Barnes in September 1978. She had known the woman for nearly sixty-five years but had avoided seeing her for the last ten. Djuna Barnes was often best talked to from a distance; the two women were in touch by telephone, but had little personal contact.

I had known Barnes for only four years, but during that short period had visited with her perhaps four hundred times and probably knew her better than anyone else in the last years of her life, even though I had not seen her for the final eleven months of it. That Berenice and I both reacted in the same way—a momentary pause, then back to work—says more about Djuna Barnes and the effect she had on those close to her than a bookshelf of biographies.

The remembrances in the memoir that follows tell a good deal about Barnes, the ideas she expressed, how she remembered events of the past and her contemporaries, what she thought of the world around her, and how she viewed herself. She discussed these matters and others during the time I knew her, repeating some of it word for word dozens of times, often attaching great importance to things that seemed trivial and relegating matters of seeming significance to nothing. She was a perplexing but ever fascinating woman.

I have attempted to trace my relationship with Barnes chronologically from my initial innocent diary entries through a developing relationship and finally to a parting of the ways. The dated diary entries that roughly chronicle our first five months were usually typed late at night after a meeting or series of meetings. I altered them slightly here, not in terms of fact but simply to make them appear less crude. The originals were done hurriedly, my only intention being to make rough notes of what had transpired at the time. I have retained items I now know to be inaccurate, and my most naive impressions, simply to retain a sense of how the relationship developed and how I learned from this extraordinarily gifted woman.

The only items I have changed are those in which Barnes was unduly harsh with someone still alive. It serves no purpose to show that at a given moment she thought ill of this person or that, people who for the most part were trying to help her in their own way. Other than these few changes, no attempt has been made to alter any of Barnes's comments, even though they may appear inaccurate or peculiar. This is what she said to me, what she presumably believed, and/or what she apparently wanted me to believe. That some of her statements may be at odds with accepted historical fact is of little consequence to me. It was how she remembered the past, her personal reality, and I'm far more interested in presenting Djuna Barnes's conception of reality than in adapting what she said or thought to any factual notions held by others.

This story began in innocence and ends in confusion. Along the way it was possible for me to learn something of the personality and mental processes of this singularly independent and mysterious woman. It was also an opportunity to witness how a vigorous mind can partially overcome the infirmities of old age, but how extreme depression and self-doubt can sap that vigor at any moment. I remain perplexed about much that transpired during the one thousand days in which I regularly saw Miss Barnes but, distressing though the relationship often became, I would willingly encounter her again.

* * *

In September 1978, Berenice Abbott was in New York City on business and telephoned to say she wanted to discuss an unusual matter with me. We met later in the day; I was then told she had been in touch with her old friend, Djuna Barnes, and was concerned about her. The word she used to describe Barnes's situation was "desperate." She was plagued with many illnesses and various problems, lived alone, had no close friends, and was ignored by her few living relatives. Her writings, papers, and business affairs were in disarray. Berenice added that many of the difficulties faced by Barnes were of her own making because she was so difficult and demanding; she had no friends, not merely because so many of them were dead, but because she was so hard to get along with on any level. She suggested that since I lived close to Barnes, was reasonably bright, and had the kind of disposition that could probably tolerate Barnes's eccentricities, I should do her a favor, make an appointment to meet with the legendary reclusive writer, and see if there was anything I might do to assist her. Berenice had even gone so far as to tell Barnes I would be in touch.

I decided to do as Berenice asked, but with some misgivings. I was well aware of Djuna Barnes's reputation and carefully considered what might be the outcome of the proposed meeting. The little I knew about Barnes was from Berenice Abbott, but it was little because Berenice is not a gossip and does not tend to discuss people. I had read *Nightwood* in college and was sufficiently impressed to buy other books by Barnes as they turned up on remainder tables in my neighborhood bookstores, but it had never occurred to me to consider these books as anything more than interesting stories, and I read them superficially. I had no idea what to expect, but three days after my meeting with Berenice I telephoned Djuna Barnes at CH3-8134, was greeted in a formal but pleasant manner, and made an appointment to meet the following day at 4:00 P.M. I told Miss Barnes I wanted to bring a friend, Liza Stelle, with me if that met with her approval. She said she would expect both of us at the appointed hour.

Patchin Place is a small, picturesque, private courtyard in Greenwich Village, in the middle of a charming block on Tenth Street between Greenwich and Avenue of the Americas. The entrance is closed off by an imposing metal gate. The north side of Tenth Street is made up of quaint, old three-story federal buildings; the Jefferson Market Court House and garden are on the south. Patchin Place itself, no more than thirty yards long, remains an island of tranquility in the swarm of shops and upper-middle-class bedrooms that is now Greenwich Village. In 1978, Djuna Barnes had known this tiny enclave for over sixty years and had lived at Number Five for almost forty.

I had walked by the guarded entrance many times during my years in the neighborhood, but had never ventured inside. The sign said it was private, and I respected the wishes of those lucky enough to live there. On this day, however, I had an invitation and with my friend, Liza, walked down the narrow sidewalk to Number Five and pressed the button marked 2F. We were buzzed in immediately and walked up a narrow, badly listing stairway to the second floor. Nothing identified Barnes's apartment; the only item in the small slot that usually held the name of an occupant was a small typewritten notice which stated "Do Not Disturb!" Years later I often wondered how different my life might have been if I'd heeded the warning of that small sign. But on that day I had been asked to disturb the occupant of 2F, and I knocked on the door.

Djuna Barnes was waiting for us; the door seemed to open the moment I struck it. We were greeted formally, asked to come in, and apologies were made about the lack of chairs. I sat down in one of the two available and couldn't help but think I was in a time capsule. Was I suddenly back in the 1920s or the 1930s? Was this the old Greenwich Village I had only read about, the way it was before everyone ran off to Paris? Or was this a remnant of Paris in the 1920s? I snapped out of these thoughts and looked at the reality of Djuna Barnes and her surroundings.

She appeared very frail; it was obviously difficult for her to stand erect, but she had taken great pains to present herself as well as possible. Her hair was freshly washed and curled, her dressing gown clean and attractive. A glance about the room, however, revealed serious disorganization. The desk was cluttered, papers piled everywhere. I sat still, taking in an impression of the room and listening to Djuna Barnes. She was very formal; perhaps correct is a better word. I had no idea of what to expect from her, but I did think the meeting would be relatively brief. It was not; Liza and I left four hours later. The conversation seemed a variation of the room in which we were sitting—it rambled and was anything but to the point.

It became obvious that Barnes was in ill health; what couldn't be noticed in a glance became apparent as the conversation progressed. She was not prone to hide any of her infirmities; quite to the contrary, she talked of them incessantly. I had somehow expected to encounter someone close-mouthed and withdrawn, but she wanted to talk. I listened intently and took in as much of my surroundings as possible, not foreseeing that I would be seeing them frequently. Following is a short description of Barnes's apartment that I wrote a few years and many visits later.

"Djuna Barnes's one-room apartment is on the second floor of Number Five Patchin Place. It is a small room, about twelve by fourteen, supplemented by the tiny bathroom, an even smaller kitchen area and a large walk-in closet. Illumination is poor; the main room has two windows and three small lamps, one on the desk, a small floor lamp by the bed and a lamp fashioned out of French carnival glass on the bureau. In other areas of the room bare lightbulbs hang from ceiling fixtures.

"The two windows overlook the narrow courtyard that is Patchin Place. Iron gates protect against potential intruders; shades and curtains offer protection from prying eyes but restrict sunlight as well. A massive rectangular table of dark brown wood is between the two windows. It is cluttered with loose papers, boxes of papers, old pencils, odds and ends, and a very old, barely working television set, its garish blue-green frame contrasting with the drab surroundings. File boxes of letters are under the table, numbered consecutively but giving no indication of the year. At any point in time there are at least fifteen or more of these boxes, their bright orange spines among the brightest objects in the room. Jammed against the table is a more proper writing space, a somewhat newer, lightly colored table. Berenice Abbott had bought it for her years ago. It is also littered with piles of papers, drafts of poems, grocery lists, old bank statements, and thousands of other scraps of paper—all saved for no apparent reason. A very old, portable typewriter sits in the middle of the table, along with stubs of pencils with ever hardening erasers, empty ball point pens, a small knife for sharpening the pencils to even shorter length, and a lifetime supply of red-and-black typewriter ribbons, new and used. Underneath this table are more boxes of papers, filled to overflowing.

"A vintage-1950s swivel chair is behind this desk; a 180-degree turn in the chair faces one toward a wall of bookcases, separated in the middle by a modest fireplace. On the right the bookcases are from floor to ceiling, the ones on the left of the fireplace, only part way up. The books are arranged in no particular order; most are worn, covered with dust, long unused. A set of English dictionaries, very old and very large, dominates a moderately accessible shelf. The fireplace is used infrequently; it has not burned wood in years, just as the books on the top shelf have forty years of accumulated dust. The fireplace burns only papers, a pile of which, ready for burning, is always at hand. Above the fireplace is a narrow mantle, crammed with odds and ends: yellowing photographs of long dead friends, a container of matches, a sherry glass, a photocopy of her painting "Alice," my photograph of Maggie Condon, a gryphon-like ceramic creature with a tail usable as a candle holder, and other assorted objects.

"A single bed, covered with a light blue blanket and piled with pillows of various sizes all the way down to a special baby pillow, is parallel to the bookcase. The foot of the bed is less than three feet from the desk. At bed level a few precious books are close at hand, but some of the shelves have been cleared for an old forties-vintage radio and an inhalation device with bottles full of doses of medicine for use with the machine. A few folders of papers, bank books, and her will are also nearby, as are special notes and last letters from T. S. Eliot. Next to the bed, on the other side, is a small oval table laden with bottles of medicine, lavender smelling salts, a blue "princess" telephone, a listing of the numbers of acquaintances (with sex, race, and religion noted), keys attached to a long ribbon, and on any given day assorted lists of groceries, medicines, and incomplete manuscripts. Under the table are boxes of tissues, aerosol cans of Hargate roach spray, an oxygen tank and additional breathing apparatus. In back of the table is an elegant walking stick, its handsome tassle hanging over the bedpost.

"Next come two small doors which lead to the walk-in closet that had previously been full of books, papers, old clothes, an easel, and a refrigerator, plugged into a light socket in the ceiling.

Now the closet contains only a small bed, ostensibly for a nurse, a chair, and the same refrigerator, still plugged into the ceiling, giving the entire space the look of a cartoon. The bookshelves now store sheets, towels, and hundreds of bottles of long since discarded medicine.

"The police-locked door to the hallway is next, then the narrow door to the tiny kitchen, wide enough for an ancient gas stove, an even smaller sink, and a few shelves crammed with assorted food-stuffs. Eating utensils are kept in drinking glasses, there being no drawers for them. Two bare bulbs hang from a double fixture, the 15-watt bulb burns continuously as a night light, the stronger bulb is used when cooking. A thin door can be closed to hide the kitchen if a visitor is present; this is a necessity because the only chair a visitor may comfortably use is placed beside this door, which, if not shut, would hide the visitor from anyone else in the room. The chair itself, an overstuffed antique armchair, had been recently upholstered, courtesy of Macy's. A chest of drawers is next, the top crammed with many objects. The bizarre carnival glass lamp burns brightly, illuminating old bottles of perfume, discarded cosmetics, an old fur hat, bric-a-brac of all sorts, and a small postcard illustrated with "Violets" by Dürer. The top, right-hand drawer holds a special treasure: buried beneath assorted clothing is a small misshapen doll from the 1890s. A small mirror above the bureau reflects the room; towards the floor are more boxes of papers, overflowing and unsorted. The bathroom door takes up the rest of this wall; the bathroom itself is twice as large as the kitchen and everything in it is also old. Besides its antiquity, the bathroom is not distinguished by anything other than its extreme heat and the toilet which, due to age and neglect, flushes spontaneously.

"The walls of the room are bare; except for the mementos on the mantel there are no photographs or paintings. Nothing in frames. The only decoration is a two-foot-high, cherub-like figure which rests on top of the bookcase near the bed. Paint flecks off its face, adding to the general feeling of deterioration. In fact, everything in the room seems in a state of decay, a room full of despair, disarray, and confusion. It appears to be a place shut away from time, but the ravages of time are there. The memories, ideas and values in this room are from many decades past."

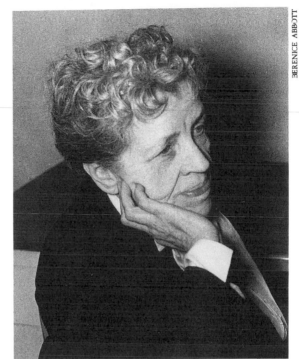

Barnes,
circa
1954

*I*n September 1978, Djuna Barnes was probably in more desperate circumstances than those indicated by Berenice Abbott. Eighty-six years had taken a physical toll; had she not possessed the constitution of an ox, she would probably have long been dead because she had once smoked to excess, was equally fond of strong drink, and was prone to deprive herself of anything that made life easier. When I first met her she was no longer smoking or drinking, but she certainly was in the first ranks of the deprivation patrol.

Her physical problems were numerous, but none seemed immediately life-threatening. She suffered from breathing difficulties—chronic emphysema—and two or three times an hour she would be racked with horrible coughing fits. Her heart was weakening; she took various medications to deal with this condition, and the nitroglycerin pills were always nearby. Arthritis and hardening of the arteries were also problems. The arthritis was, obviously, not treatable, but the arteries were, in her mind, being maintained by a salt-free diet. Adding to these complications were the cataracts on both eyes; she was virtually blind in one eye and was able to read through the other partially clouded eye only by means of a large magnifying glass. To add to the misery of a restricted, salt-free diet was the difficulty she had in eating anything solid. Her false teeth had been badly fitted, and there was virtually no ridge upon which to fit a new set.

All these problems were a source of constant worry and complaint, but only one thing truly terrified her: blindness. If she was unable to see, she could not do any work, could not finish the scattered poems that littered her desk. But it was the almost constant pain that caused her the most immediate agony. The source of the pain was arthritis of the spine, even though Barnes was convinced it was cancer of the rectum. Adding to the arthritis pain was a self-inflicted horror: as a young girl Barnes had been advised by her grandmother that proper ladies always made use of a warm water enema to empty their bowels, and so the natural elasticity and functioning of her bowels was a memory. This, of course, added to the pain brought on by arthritis and, not surprisingly, her concern about cancer of the rectum.

Darvon was the primary remedy for the pain; she'd been taking it for years even though it produced no particular relief. This medication did, however, cause the side-effects so frequently associated with it: irritability, confusion, and sometimes irrational behavior. She was taking other drugs, at least half a dozen on a regular daily basis, but the darvon was the one that caused most of the side-effects. Considering her physical problems, the medication she was taking, and her appalling diet, it was amazing that she could remember from one day to the next, let alone do any meaningful work. But she could remember most of the important matters at hand and was, in fact, witty, articulate, highly intelligent, and seemingly capable of working on her poetry if only some of her problems could be solved.

The problems stretched far beyond simple physical difficulties. The small apartment in which she had lived for forty years, while reasonably tidy and as clean as possible, was in fact a shambles, with poems written in the middle of grocery lists, and with no organization in the paper clutter everywhere. Working on a poem, she seemed to lack the ability to begin where she had left off the day before; she would date a page and start again from the beginning. The results were hundreds of versions of the same poem in various states of completion; a mixture of some very old with some done the day before. That she was visually impaired made it extremely difficult for her to bring any order to the confusion caused by her work habits. This was, of course, frustrating, and combined with the constant pain and confusion brought on by the drugs, it led to a seemingly hopeless situation in her mind. And this was, presumably, why she turned to one of her few remaining friends, Berenice Abbott, and in so doing allowed an outsider to enter the apartment that had been so long off-limits to almost everyone.

There were, naturally, other problems. Correspondence was not attended to on a regular basis, her copyrights in the U.S. and abroad were confused, most of her writing was out of print everywhere, and her modest savings were not being utilized in the best fashion.

She was by no means destitute; she had slightly over $100,000 in four different saving banks in Greenwich Village, but for the most part lived on her minimal social security check, about $115 per month, and a monthly stipend of $300 from Peggy Guggenheim, which had been coming for years and continued even after Guggenheim's death. The funds she had in the various banks simply sat there, at the lowest possible interest; no one had ever advised her that she should perhaps seek a higher rate at the bank and not knowing about such things, it didn't occur to her that she should. This alone indicated her estrangement from the outside world, even from her own family. One of her brothers, still alive, had once been an officer of a major New York City bank, and while his sister's money sat earning simple interest, he remained silent.

The money Barnes had saved came from two sources: she had sold the major portion of her papers and letters, along with some rare books, to the University of Maryland in the early 1970s. This sale provided for most of the money on hand; the rest was her frugality. Her expenses were modest: an apartment that cost about $110 per month, a tiny telephone bill, an equally small electricity charge, medicine, and a little food. She had virtually no other expenses. She bought no newspapers, subscribed to nothing other than the *Times Literary Supplement*, and purchased no books. She rarely left her apartment, except occasionally to visit a doctor, which was usually paid for by Medicaid and Medicare.

Barnes's friends were, for the most part, long dead or lived far from New York City. The few still alive—Abbott, Guggenheim,

Janet Flanner—while genuinely concerned about Barnes, were far away in Maine, Venice, and Paris. It was difficult to maintain a friendship with Barnes, but it was easier if a considerable distance was involved. There were, of course, a few people who saw her: the daughter of an old friend, an editor who had arranged for the reissue of *Ladies Almanack* in the early 1970s, a cleaning boy who arrived punctually once a week, and a middle-aged man, who, though something of a collector of elderly female writers, was, nonetheless, genuinely fond of Barnes. None of these people, except the cleaning boy, saw her more than a few times a year, and she did not wish to entrust them with any of her serious affairs. Perhaps she was ashamed to ask; certainly those who occasionally visited were disinclined to offer, not because of a lack of good intentions but because of their fear of offending Barnes. Even her relatives remained out of the picture; she once said that Saxon, her brother, had visited her but once in seventeen years, even though he did talk to her regularly on the telephone and occasionally sent her gifts she regarded as useless. He lived about two hours from New York City.

Barnes might have had as much help as she wanted; with a few telephone calls it would have been possible to line up volunteers the length of Patchin Place to look in on her regularly, but the mystery she had so consciously cultivated for so many years ruled out such a possibility. Even if there had been no such mystery her pride would have prevented any outside assistance. So she was alone, by choice as much as by circumstance. She valued her independence as much as Cyrano valued his white plume; indeed, pride, independence, solitude, and anger at a world she neither understood nor wished to be a part of were all that kept her going at the end of her life. She stated this eloquently time and time again.

Later in the evening, after our first meeting, I found myself perplexed. Why should an individual of such high intelligence and ability find herself in such a desperate situation? Something was obviously wrong, I thought. It was clear that I didn't know enough, that there was much more to Miss Barnes's plight than met the eye. At the same time the practical side of my nature recognized that it would be relatively simple to clear up some of her more pressing needs. My own life was very complicated at the time, but I felt it would take little effort to try to attend to some of Barnes's more immediate problems. I planned to tell Berenice Abbott about the meeting, and I decided to make the time to call Barnes once a week to be of whatever assistance might be possible.

Barnes,
circa
late
1940s
in New
York

Once this decision was made, I went down to Canal Street and bought Barnes an inexpensive, simple cassette tape recorder. Then I made some cassettes of Dylan Thomas reading his works and her *Nightwood*. She had been in the audience when Thomas read *Under Milk Wood* at the 92nd Street YMHA in the early 1950s. I thought it might be a treat for her to hear him once again.

Four days after our first meeting, I telephoned Barnes from the corner of Greenwich and Tenth Street and said I'd like to pay a visit. She seemed pleased and suggested I come by immediately. Over the next few months, through 3 February 1979, I met with her approximately three times a week. At the end of most of these meetings, I typed informal notes on our conversations, her comments, and how her work was progressing. There is little analysis in these comments, but they do present a brief, though sustained, account of the development of our relationship.

19 September 1978

First meeting with Djuna Barnes at 4:30. I took Liza Stelle with me for protection. The meeting was arranged by Berenice Abbott, who evidenced much concern for her old friend who, she said, was facing very difficult times.

Djuna Barnes remains an extremely handsome woman. She is very old and her physical problems have her down a bit, particularly the fear of blindness, but her mind is sharp and she is as interesting a conversationalist as I have ever encountered. I planned to stay an hour and simply offer whatever assistance Liza and I might be able to provide. We stayed and talked for more than four hours.

Her book, *Nightwood*, is on her mind. She says things like "Isn't it simply a beautiful work" and "I wonder how I could have written it." She feels she would be unable to write it now and says she hasn't even looked at it for years. She tries to give the impression she hasn't looked at anything she has written for some time, but she did say she had recently reread *A Night Among the Horses* and didn't think it was very good.

Miss Barnes is annoyed with the people at Caedmon Records because of their release of a record that includes Dylan Thomas reading an excerpt from *Nightwood*. She's happy to have Thomas reading from her work, though she insists he should have asked her permission, but she's angry because Caedmon claims the record is not selling. How can that be, she wonders. Eight people have asked her for movie rights and someone "associated with Mr. Papp" has even approached her about turning the book into a play. She has refused all these offers, but it proves to her that there is keen interest in the book. It follows, therefore, in her mind, that a record of Dylan Thomas reading from the book should sell briskly.

She gives the impression of not being opposed to an adaptation of *Nightwood*, but only if she can do the job. She is much more concerned with a production of her play, *The Antiphon*, which is being planned in Switzerland. There are a number of problems, the foremost being the translation of the play into German. There being two different editions of the play, the man scheduled to direct does not approve of either and wishes to translate the play himself. Miss Barnes is in a quandary because she does not speak or read German (or any other foreign language). She's in favor of a production, but she is unable to be of any assistance in moving the project forward and is bogged down with paper work and correspondence concerning it.

She spoke at length about Joyce (Jim) and how he would read *Ulysses* to her aloud, and about T. S. Eliot (Tom) as well. At one point she became very angry and raged about a small bookstore on Tenth Street called Djuna Books. She is outraged by its existence. "How dare they," she said, adding, "it is probably a terrible little lesbian bookshop." Other matters of less passionate concern are her simple daily existence, various doctors, the effort it takes to bring the mail upstairs, a young man who cleans her room once a week, and her love of a mixture of coffee ice cream and ginger ale. She is limited in what she can do, what she can eat, where she can go, and whom she sees, but she is terribly bright and very interesting. It will be an adventure chatting with her.

23 September

My second meeting with Djuna Barnes. This time I merely telephoned from the corner and went by. She had not curled her hair and was not in her best dressing gown as had been the case a few days earlier. She had not expected me and was not prepared for a visitor, but agreed to see me, apparently convinced I was not a rascal. We talked for a long time about many things.

I took her the small cassette tape recorder and two cassettes of Dylan Thomas reading. She was certain she did not want to listen, but I played one anyway. The moment she heard Thomas's voice she broke into a wide smile and didn't say a word until he finished reading *Fern Hill*. It was apparent she knew the poem well and a moment after its conclusion expressed an interest in learning how to operate the "infernal little machine." She is obviously torn between wanting me to take it away and wanting to listen further. She said she had done nothing for so long that it might be a problem to do something. I showed how easy the machine is to operate and made an effort to portray it as enjoyable, explaining it is simple for me to transfer recordings to cassettes with all the equipment at my recording studio. I asked what she liked in music; she replied she prefers "old-fashioned" music, by which she means François Couperin and Claudio Monteverdi. She asked about John Cage and we discussed him. When I told her about his class in picking mushrooms, she laughed. She feels his music is nonsense and doesn't like it at all. She also dislikes Frank Sinatra and feels "he is not a nice man." This must be one of the few times Cage and Sinatra have been so close. The conversation about recording ended with my asking what she might like to hear, adding I had a recording of an excerpt from *Ulysses*. This did interest her and prompted a question as to whether Joyce made any recording himself. I said I thought he had and would make an attempt to find it. She is obviously interested in the tape recorder.

We discussed current events and it is clear that Miss Barnes is not well-informed. She no longer receives any magazines or newspapers other than the (London) *Times Literary Supplement*. She doesn't read the *New York Times* or any other news publications, but does listen to the radio a good deal and, on some occasions, listens to television, which she can barely see. Inflation is a concern, and she is certain the country is going to the dogs. There are few interesting politicians; Harry Truman was "not that good" and "poor Jack Kennedy" were two she mentioned briefly. Current events are just not of much concern.

But writing, her writing, is of concern. She considers "Aller et Retour" and "The Passion" to be her best stories. Someone apparently issued a small pirated book entitled *Vagaries Malicieux*; it contains two of her stories, but she has never seen a copy and would like to someday. Things like this happen to her all the time. Many of her stories were in newspapers and old magazines; people do as they please and just take them. The same holds true for a 1948 edition of *The Book of Repulsive Women*. It is a pirated version and she hates it, like all the other pirated books.

Miss Barnes is equally unhappy with all the people who are forever pestering her for information about herself, about almost everything that has ever been written about her, and the people who annoy her friends looking for bits of scandal and gossip. It seems, based on her comments, that many "literary" people, i.e., people who are interested in those who write, have been unpleasant to her and that she has been stern with them in return. She speaks disparagingly of people who want to record her, how they paw through her bookshelves and, on occasion, take books, saying things like "you must have many copies of this one!" I find it hard to believe she'd allow this to happen, but I'm equally certain people do annoy her a great deal, and she dislikes it intensely. All the while she is unhappy that there are not many of her friends alive; apparently she'd enjoy being "annoyed" by them.

She asked about *The Antiphon*. I said I thought it was a very difficult play and had not looked at it for about nine years. It is obvious she wished to discuss it. Do I have a copy? Might I reread it? What edition do I have? She says the U.K. edition is the first version but the second, in *Selected Works*, is superior. Why some people are negative about *The Antiphon* puzzles her. T. S. Eliot apparently told her he did not like the play but thought the last act was the best piece of theatrical writing he had ever read. She is unhappy that it has not been produced in the United States and remains concerned about the possibly-forthcoming Swiss/German production.

She claims to be working hard on her poetry, but has been unable to make as much progress as she had believed possible. Though she wants to get a short book of poems together, her failing eyesight is a great hindrance. The poems are scattered about and she can't see well enough to put all the pieces together. She holds some of her poetry in low regard; there is little she feels is first-rate. Is this an excuse to abandon it altogether? Yet, she works on the poetry daily. I told her that all she really needs is adequate eyesight. She desperately wants to find a doctor who might save or improve her sight. I told her I'll try to assist in finding such a doctor, and failing that I'd find her an "Eric Fenby." She didn't understand and I told her the story of how Fenby aided the blind Frederick Delius. She said she didn't like Delius at all and I told her that was completely irrelevant. I think she wants to work, but needs a good doctor to tend to her failing vision. It will be a challenge to find the proper specialist.

27, 29 September

We discussed many things: most importantly how to get her finances in order, a simple matter, and a preliminary eye examination. An appointment is set for 6 October with Dr. Milton Zaret, a man with fine credentials.

Miss Barnes's copyrights are also a matter of immediate concern. Few of her short stories have any protection at all, so anyone may do with them as they please. An Italian publisher wishes to issue "Spillway" and is offering a seven hundred dollar advance. He is also prepared to pay one thousand dollars for *Nightwood*. She signed both contracts and I posted them.

I played a cassette of Joyce reading "Anna Livia Plurabelle" from *Finnegan's Wake*. The recording quality is very poor, but it pleased Miss Barnes; it caused her to talk about him at length. She says it is important to have Joyce reading himself because he often told her *Finnegan's Wake* is meant to be read aloud. He told her the book should never be read by the person who purchases it; it should be read aloud by that person to someone else. She told of Joyce reading to her and then she telling him she didn't understand one word of it but it sounded very funny. Joyce apparently told her she was exactly right; the book was funny and meant to amuse; he wished more people reacted the same way. She also told how Joyce was interested in rivers and gathered as much information as possible about the rivers of the world. His rooms were full of atlases, and he was very concerned about the relationship of the rhythmic flow of his books with the flow of rivers.

Music was also important to Joyce, which may be seen in the way he used words. Miss Barnes listened to Joyce's poems on the cassette. She says he was not a good poet, that his early work was romantic and sentimental. She claims Joyce's wife, Nora, used to tell her she "should have known him when he was younger," that he was nothing like the man he was in the 1920s. Nora Joyce also told her over and over that no one should ever associate her with Molly Bloom.

Miss Barnes then asked if I could find the cassette of Dylan Thomas reading *Nightwood*. She had somehow misplaced it. I found it in a box of papers; things move about this room in a strange fashion. She listened carefully as Thomas read the lines; she interrupted twice, then she said he read a line incorrectly. She must have a perfect notion of what she wrote so long ago.

She likes Thomas's performance but also feels it is perhaps high-minded. She spoke of her own voice and how bad it sounds, which is why she has never consented to make any recordings. I suggested it does not sound so bad and she should at least consider making a recording. She says she is unable to remember one verse she has ever written; this seems unlikely since not five minutes earlier she remembered *Nightwood* sufficiently well to take notice of some minor mistakes by Dylan Thomas. I think I will try to persuade her to at least attempt a recording.

I'd mentioned that the day before I'd come upon a copy of *A Book* in a used bookstore. She asked that I bring it by; it had been many years since she had seen a copy. I brought it today and she eagerly looked at all the drawings, identifying the people she used for the illustrations. One was an actress, another a "pansy," a third the wife of Max Eastman. She feels the drawing of Eastman's wife is good, but many of her earliest drawings were poor and most were burned. I asked her to sign my copy and she did so without hesitation, while telling a convoluted story about a man who wanted to issue a book of her poems in a fancy edition and have her sign one hundred copies. He offered her one dollar for each signature. She told the man to go to hell. She began to skim through the book and suddenly stopped at a story (or poem) and said, "After I published this one they first accused me of being a lesbian." She added that the accusation was nonsense.

We spoke about other writers, such as Knut Hamsun and J. M. Synge, both of whom she enjoyed long ago but doesn't care for now. She still enjoys Keats and one book by Ford Madox Ford; she claims the only Ford worth reading is *No More Parades*. This is handy; it's the only one I own.

We also discussed her books and various copyright problems associated with them. Liveright held all the early copyrights and she has only recently regained control. Many people have wanted to republish *Ryder*, but the copyright problem prevented it because whoever is left in the Liveright firm said they would make trouble. She said an unpleasant man from Viking once came by to discuss republishing the book, but she threw him out. She says, however, she is not opposed to a reissue and gave me permission to cast about for a suitable publisher willing to do a good job.

The rest of our conversations were about trivial matters. She says she wants to show me an album of old photographs. She also pointed out a small, framed, postcard-sized print of violets by Dürer that was given to her by a man whom she was engaged to marry "for about twelve days."

6 October

The day for the appointment with Dr. Milton Zaret. Miss Barnes didn't want to get dressed but finally agreed to go. His diagnosis is that the previous five doctors were wrong, and he prescribed glasses that should enable adequate sight in the right eye. She is not in as bad shape as the other doctors suggested; Dr. Zaret says he can even operate in six months if the right eye fails because there is nothing wrong with the left except cataracts. A successful day: we almost didn't go because of the slight rain.

The long drive to Dr. Zaret's office afforded much time to talk. It had been some time since Miss Barnes ventured so far from Patchin Place; she looked about in wonderment and asked many questions about where we were and when this or that building was constructed. As her amazement waned she spoke of there being so many dreadful writers who are well paid. She says the royalties on her books in the United States came to $3.09 for 1977. This is the exact figure she stated. I find it hard to believe. She is proud of never writing anything for popular consumption and still refuses to have some of her work reprinted, even though people send her money when they request permission. She feels that if she accepts money, it will imply a measure of approval. She does not wish to be a part of any such schemes. Of course, she needs the money and claims to have sold some of her possessions in the past, such as an inscribed copy of *Ulysses* for a mere $150.

She spoke of Jean Cocteau: "He was a pansy, surrounded by a lot of other pansies but he was clever." She loves his movies and took the time to describe the one she likes best: *Blood of a Poet.* This film led to Lee Miller and in turn to Man Ray. She says Man Ray once took a good photograph of her with Myrna Loy. I have never seen it; perhaps I will someday. She then described several scenes from *The Eternal Return.* When she discovered I had not seen it, she stopped.

Miss Barnes once enjoyed the movies; she says she used to go to them all the time, but she stopped when she was no longer able to walk well. She began to fear going out at night. Someone once tried to break into her room while she was asleep, but she woke up, went to the window as the intruder was attempting to enter, and hit him over the head with a stick. The police arrived later and praised her bravery, but urged her not to ever buy a pistol because she'd probably use it. She says she is much braver in her own room than she could ever be on the street. Suddenly she switched back to Cocteau; she mentioned Raymond Radiguet and how she had once written a story about him. She didn't say which it was and, foolishly, I didn't ask her to identify it.

Miss Barnes then began talking about Alfred Stieglitz, perhaps because she's aware I'm interested in photography. She claims he was perfectly horrible to Georgia O'Keeffe; he never touched her at all. He wanted a young person around for the sake of his ego, and he told her to put all of her sexual energy into her painting.

Nightwood came up again. After the book was released, everyone thought she was a lesbian; she claims if she'd known that would happen, she would never have written it. I told her that it didn't make any difference whether someone thinks she is a lesbian, and she agreed, but said it does bother her and then became very angry at the use of her name by Djuna Books. She says she is a very old-fashioned lady with very old-fashioned values, adding how terrible it is that all the girls these days sleep with boys to whom they are not married.

18 October

The new glasses work well and Miss Barnes has not called very often. I telephoned her and went by. She is concerned about disposing of some of her papers that are of interest to the University of Maryland. She has already willed them to the university but feels a sale now might generate a little money. She asked me to sort through them; she feels almost all the papers are of a business nature but would like to make certain. I told her it was not a problem and can probably be done very quickly. She says the university wants every scrap of paper she has, to leave her with as little as possible. A man from the university library is apparently scheduled to make a visit at the end of the month. His purpose seems to be to haul everything away, and Miss Barnes said, "Let's not let him."

All these papers are of great concern. Miss Barnes is worried about how an executor might handle them if she makes no specific provisions. Her present executor is the daughter of her lawyer, who is apparently very old. She is not even certain he is still alive, and she is most apprehensive about sorting out this problem.

We had a short discussion about *The Antiphon*. When I told her the actor Michael Moriarty had expressed interest in reading from *Ryder*, she wondered whether he might consider her play. It is a possibility. She told me the names of some of the people in *Nightwood*. Thelma Wood is Robin, Henriette Metcalf is Nora, and Dan Mahoney is Dr. O'Connor. She said the old photograph, clipped from a magazine sitting next to the sixty-year-old Kodak brownie, is of the critic Edwin Muir. I wonder who else was photographed by that old camera once upon a time. I told Miss Barnes I was off to Maine, but would call when I return on 25 October.

25 October

Miss Barnes is feeling badly: trouble with her lungs, but mentally very spirited. She is pleased with the photographs of James Joyce and herself that Berenice sent, but is even happier with all the groceries. She insists on paying for everything, down to the last penny.

She is very puzzled by Berenice and asked many questions about what she does with her time and how she copes with old age. I don't think she is necessarily concerned about Berenice, but is more interested in her circumstances. She claims Berenice dressed her up for the photograph; this is interesting for Berenice says exactly the opposite, that Barnes was more concerned about luxurious dress than anyone in her crowd, except possibly for Margaret Anderson. She studied both photographs carefully and related a story about how one magazine had retouched a photograph of her, turning a dime store ring into an emerald. She also told a tale of how Joyce had once asked her to buy him a particular iron ring, but she was poor and could not do so. She added he didn't need the ring, that Berenice's photograph shows clearly he's already wearing two on one hand. She loves Joyce's books, but feels that he was a great burden to those who knew him well and that his wife Nora was a martyr to his writing.

Miss Barnes has taken an interesting position with regard to my placing *Ryder*. She says it is a good enough book and a "bestseller" when it was originally issued but is, nonetheless, an immature work. She claims not to care if it is reissued or not, and she seems sincere. It may be she is preparing herself for rejection; she is not opposed to my continuing the search.

Dan Mahoney became the subject of our conversation; he appears in *Ryder* before *Nightwood*. People used to follow him about, trying to write down what he said. There was even a man who approached him after *Nightwood* was issued and suggested Mahoney just talk and talk and that way there could be another *Nightwood*-type book. In this discussion of Mahoney, Miss Barnes brought up the Dylan Thomas reading. I told her I'd seen the Welsh National Theater Company do *Under Nightwood* a few months earlier. I quickly caught my mistake and said *Under Milk Wood*, and she laughed loudly, saying, "Don't worry, it's the same thing." Thomas once told her the only writing he really liked was Shakespeare's, Marlowe's, and *Nightwood*. She is certain he didn't mean it, but it was nice to hear.

Miss Barnes then took a swipe at lesbians, expanding on her feelings about women in general and lesbians in particular. She claims to hate lesbians and is rather unfeeling towards women, but she did love Thelma Wood in a strong and passionate way, primarily because Thelma reminded her of her grandmother. Thelma looked just like her grandmother who often protected her from an abusive father, who enjoyed beating her with a whip. The grandmother, she says, kept him from doing it too often. She said all this very quickly and didn't make much of it; it seems she wanted to make the point that she cared for Thelma Wood very much, but is not a lesbian and doesn't particularly have strong sexual feelings about women. She added, almost as an afterthought, that women are often too sloppy and sentimental for her, and men usually are not and therefore they are of more interest.

She has been reading Louis Kannenstine's *The Art of Djuna Barnes* and feels it is adequate even though it contains a number of inaccuracies. She has been talking with him, and he's writing a book about Paris in the 1920s and wishes to alter anything he might have said about her that is inaccurate. She doesn't want him to change anything and asked me if I thought she should even bother looking at the manuscript. I told her, of course, that Kannenstine is making an effort to be honorable. She's upset about a story he put in the book about her being able to hit a spittoon from one hundred feet. The story is actually about someone else, but the columnist Walter Winchell claimed it was about her, and it stuck. She said, "Why bother to change it after all this time?"

The Swiss director, Werner Duggelin, has replied regarding the translation of *The Antiphon*. He is willing to do whatever is necessary to secure permission to mount the play; perhaps this is why she is so optimistic at our meeting today. It was the best to date.

26 October

The spare glasses from The Eye Shop are ready; now there will be two to be misplaced. Jussi Korzenlowski, Miss Barnes's hired boy, was there working when I arrived. He is about fifty and uninterested in literary matters. He enjoys working for Miss Barnes; he washes and cleans the floor on his knees, reaching into places where no foot ever rests. He prefers to use a bucket of water and an old rag to do the job. I find this a little peculiar. He left about 6:00; Miss Barnes and I talked until after 9:00.

Hart Crane was a little terror in Paris. The first time he called, he left a note on her door hanging from a dagger. She thinks he is a good poet, more than adequate but not top drawer. His parents were forever sending candies to Margaret Anderson; some of them were passed along to Miss Barnes. I had a Walker Evans book in my bag and decided to point out the photograph of Crane; she finds it, like Crane's poems, adequate but in no way distinguished. She made a point to say he did not jump off that boat because of Peggy Cowley; he was gay, so that certainly couldn't have been the reason. I'm surprised she used the word "gay": it was the first time.

Now that the battle over *The Antiphon* is won, doubt has set in over the translation again. I urged her to use whatever translation the director feels is best. The translation by "the two girls" is the difficulty. She is afraid it is not good. "The two girls" are lesbians who bring her flowers and candy and think she is so divine, and she can't stand it. The point was made again about hating lesbians; they are all "so boring."

She doesn't want to offend "the two girls" but thinks their translation will probably be mushy. Then she brought up copyrights. Who holds them? I told her she holds the copyrights to both editions. I think she finally understands; she told me to write Duggelin, the Swiss director, and tell him to mount the play but to make certain he doesn't use a mushy translation. She then told me he wants to make a movie of *Nightwood*. I said I didn't think this was a very good idea; let him finish the play first and then worry about a movie, making certain she remembers he is a director of plays, not motion pictures. She is very fond of Duggelin but agrees with this approach.

Man Ray caught it today. Miss Barnes claimed to have had many photographs by him but threw them away. I told her this is unfortunate; they are worth a great deal today. She feels Man Ray was very shallow, not an important artist. He was not serious, had no training, and was always doing silly things like putting tacks on an iron. He charged a great deal to do a portrait, and no one liked him but the model Kiki. So much for Man Ray.

Next subject: old people. She hates them. She hated them when she was young and she hates them now. Everyone hates old ladies because they aren't good for anything. They aren't pretty and they can't screw, so what good are they?

A man from Australia is writing a biography, and she is concerned about it. He has offered one thousand dollars to use some quotations from her books, but she will not accept it; she doesn't need one thousand dollars that much. She is primarily upset because he is running all over the world talking to everyone who ever knew her, seeking gossip and information. "Thank goodness most of my friends are dead!"

She asked to look at the Walker Evans book, *First and Last*. She knew Evans, but can't recall the circumstances in which they met or when. She looked at each photograph very carefully, turning the pages slowly. She found the book interesting but judged only one photograph exceptional, the rear view of the family plot in Kentucky (p. 158). The next photograph, the side view of the same scene, bothered her because she felt the sun was not correct; Evans should have waited until the light was right. She asked that I compare Evans with Abbott. She understood the difference but does not care for Evans's photograph of Berenice.

Susan Sontag is ill, and Miss Barnes is upset about it; she is even more concerned because she never let her come by and visit. She once told a friend to tell Sontag that if she ever saw her on the street to stop and have a chat, but this annoyed Sontag so they never got together. How complicated for something so simple.

She made one more comment about how dreadful her voice has become; it is old and wheezing with asthma. She only likes readings by Dylan Thomas and does not care for Richard Burton, T. S. Eliot, or anyone else.

I told her Les Pockell at St. Martin's has expressed an interest in *Ryder*. I am told to take one of her copies of the book and give it to him to read; since it is only "mildly dirty," it will probably be of little interest and will not sell, but she is willing to let him have a look.

Nightwood should be a movie, she thinks, but no one will be allowed to do it unless they do it perfectly, and since there are no good American directors it will never be made in this country. The movie should be in black and white and shot in and around Paris. She once rejected thirty thousand dollars for a one-year option. I find this hard to believe. Her quote for the day: "If you can't be marvelous, why bother, and you can't be marvelous very often." The one good photograph in *First and Last* proves this point in her mind. Only one of Evans's photographs is "truly marvelous."

27 October

We discussed *Ladies Almanack* today. She wrote it for fun; it was just a lark and it is not even in copyright. A good portion of it was written in a hospital while she was tending Thelma Wood, and there was not even a plan to publish it until Robert McAlmon read it and said he would pay for the printing. Miss Barnes says McAlmon did pay for the printing, but she paid for printing the illustrations. Perhaps she means he paid for the typography; it doesn't make sense the way she explains it. Nonetheless, at some point there was a disagreement with the publisher, Edward Titus, who wanted half the money for each copy sold, including those sold by Miss Barnes to friends or in cafes. She told him where to get off.

The drawings in the book are very derivative; a volume of French folk drawings published in Paris in 1925 proves the point. She says that when the book was first published she was constantly bothered by a "dreary, old lesbian named Natalie Barney" who was always after her. Barney, she claims, was a failed writer who came from a wealthy American family (a monopoly in the toilet seat business). Barney couldn't stand it if a woman rejected her. She was, apparently, a rather successful lover of ladies who usually got whomever she went after, but she didn't get Miss Barnes, or so she says. She signed my copy of the book, finding it interesting that I have the last copy, number one thousand. There is always a story when she signs a book; today it was about a man who sent her a number of bookplates to sign, but she threw them in the garbage can. "My signature is worth ten dollars. Why should I send that money to him?" The reissue of the book is an accurate facsimile; the only change is the new introduction.

We discussed her style of writing. She thinks it is amusing when people talk of her unique and wonderful style of punctuation. It is neither unique nor wonderful, she explains. She simply doesn't know any of the rules or how anything should be punctuated. She likes to use colons; they look nice. She used one in her poem, "Quarry," which was published in *The New Yorker.* The poetry editor of the magazine said she had not used a colon properly and insisted it be removed. Reluctantly, she agreed, but when it was reprinted in another publication she made certain the colon was back in its rightful place.

Miss Barnes talks a good deal about her inability to spell many words properly and her poor punctuation but does not question her ability to write at all. One thing has nothing to do with the other, and she is proud of the good things she has written, as she feels they are very well written.

It is amazing to me that she has read so much and has such retention: major and minor writers, all sorts of subjects. She asked if I had any books in my bag; I had a copy of *Major Barbara*. To her mind it is a rotten play; most of Shaw's plays are very poor, but some of his introductions are exceptional. It seems to me I've heard that before. She asked that I read her a bit of the introduction, and when I came to the point where Shaw mentions an English writer, Charles Lever, she stopped me. She was just thinking of Lever the other day, but could not think of his first name and is happy to be reminded.

"I wonder why I wrote so little," she said. "But as Tom said, some of it was marvelous." She is not fond of T. S. Eliot's poetry but feels his literary criticism is the finest in the English language. She cared for him very much personally; he was well-read, well-spoken, well-dressed, and civilized. She does not like Auden's poetry but feels sorry for him because he became so ugly: "a face like an elephant's ass."

A short conversation about surrealist painters ensued, brought about by a dust jacket that had been designed by Delvaux, whom she likes very much. She is no longer fond of Salvador Dali; he is just a prostitute. She recalled a luncheon at 21 with Janet Flanner and Anita Loos. Dali was two tables away and at one point rose and grandly announced, "All hail, Djuna Barnes!" She did not elaborate on the story other than to say she felt like hiding under the table but did not do so.

She asked me, for no immediately apparent reason, "Do you remember the ending of *Nightwood?*" I replied I did, and she then became very upset discussing this part of the book. People say Robin is making love to the dog; this is nonsense. There was nothing like that in her mind when she wrote the scene. In fact, it was taken from a real life situation she observed. A friend of hers,

Fitzie, was "drunk as a hoot and crawling around on all fours and her dog, Buff, was running around growling and barking." She spoke of how animals become confused and excited when they see their masters in an "unusual" state. She then gave her opinions on how animals feel, how people feel, and how their reactions to certain situations are based on "things they really don't know but simply feel from long, long ago, like the way children like to see the wolf in bed in *Little Red Riding Hood.*" This is right out of *Nightwood.*

Nightwood was rejected in the United States well before it came out in England. It was taken to the U.K. because some friends pushed very hard for its acceptance. Later, T. S. Eliot's introduction helped the book in the United States, but, she feels, he should have mentioned that he didn't write one for the first edition and why he did not. She did not elaborate as to why he didn't write the introduction in the beginning. She still thinks the book will make a good movie someday; perhaps Ingmar Bergman is the right director. She likes his movies, particularly *The Seventh Seal* and the *Virgin Spring.* She saw all his movies "until a few years ago when I stopped going out." The rape scene in the *Virgin Spring* is the finest thing she has ever seen in a movie, but she enjoys Bergman primarily because his ideas about God and religion are very similar to her own.

Miss Barnes is very worried about her physical condition. She speaks of seven operations, three broken ribs, a broken shoulder (e.e. cummings crawled through her window when this occurred), a pinched nerve in her spine that causes constant pain, a weak heart, crippling arthritis, lungs filled with emphysema, dreadful dietary restrictions, and oncoming blindness caused by cataracts. She asked me to get her a copy of Susan Sontag's book, *Illness as Metaphor.*

30 October

A hurried visit with little to discuss except the letter I had written
to Werner Duggelin, the director of the Schauspielhaus in Zurich.
She approves of the letter, but feels it may be a bit grand and wants
to think about it before it is posted. We had a short conversation
about various English writers, among them James Boswell and
John Aubrey. She was most interested in the production made from
Aubrey's *Brief Lives*, which I had seen a year or so ago. She wished
she could have seen it, but hadn't even known of it.

1 November

She wants the letter sent to Duggelin, but is concerned about how
the various concerned parties will react to it. I made copies for
everyone and sent them off to Switzerland, Italy, and England. At
one point she referred to Mrs. Hobbs in *The Antiphon* as "mother,"
mentioned a poem about animals she is working on, and explained
a dispute she was having with Flanner about Eliot. Flanner has
been saying (in a convoluted fashion) that she (Barnes) is a much
finer writer than Eliot. This is confusing, but the good news is that
Miss Barnes says she felt fifty years old and worked all day.

2 November

This was an interesting afternoon. Miss Barnes showed me an old
scrapbook that has the look of not having been opened for years and

years. It is in no particular order, but the last photographs are from the early forties or late thirties, and the first are from the teens. At least 80 percent of the photographs are of Thelma Wood. There is a fine copy of Berenice's portrait of Wood, plus one of Wood and Berenice together with a notation of 1921. There is a fine Man Ray portrait, a candid one of Miss Barnes on the street with Charlie Chaplin, assorted literary folks, a portrait of Constantin Brancusi signed "To Djuna Barnes," and some amusing photos of her newspaper days: being force fed, hugging a gorilla, being carried down a building by a fireman. She says she did all these crazy things for the paper to earn money for her family, which was having a poor time of it in those days.

There is also a nice snapshot of her with Mina Loy and a poor one with Natalie Barney. There is a series from the place where she lived in Algiers—"where the rent was five dollars a month and servants were five cents a day." I wonder where all the negatives might be for these wonderful old photographs. In addition to the photos, there are a few drawings by her and other people she liked and a few clippings. One is from the *New York News*, presumably from the 1920s, and is captioned "our own Gertrude Stein." She hates Stein very much.

She told me about her animal poems. There are twenty-six verses, one for each letter of the alphabet. She has been working on them a long time and they are about finished. She worked on them yesterday when she felt so well. I suggested it might be interesting to have a little drawing with each verse, and she agreed this might be charming. I told her an artist named Edward Gorey might be perfect for the project. She does not know his work; I said I'd bring her a book and if she likes the drawings, I'll ask Allegra Kent, the ballerina, whom Gorey had watched night after night at the New

York City Ballet, to contact him. Miss Barnes showed me all the drafts of the poems; there seem to be seventeen versions and they need sorting. I'll do this on Friday if she wants.

We talked about writers; it's what she enjoys best. She loves Sherlock Holmes and Conan Doyle, and she told me I should read *Anatomy of Melancholy* and *Lady Windermere's Fan*, a peculiar juxtaposition. What do I think of Lawrence Durrell and Truman Capote? She was once asked to pose with Capote, but wouldn't even consider it because he looked so stupid, the way he lounged about and had such funny looking hair. She feels he squandered his talent. A quick remark about the Gotham Book Mart and how they tried to arrange a gathering at which she would talk about Joyce. She refused their invitation, claiming she is "one person who plans to keep her remembrances of Joyce to herself." They never bothered her again about this, but did try to buy all her books.

Again, an aside about her punctuation: "It is no mystery at all. It is totally out of ignorance."

She showed me a booklet that was issued in honor of her eightieth birthday. There is a variant of the Abbott portrait on the front; Miss Barnes is grinning broadly and she hates it. I'm not surprised; it is the poorest of the series, and I'm puzzled that anyone would select it for a tribute.

Miss Barnes is worried about not being alive much longer. At one point she said, "Don't think for a minute this is the real Djuna Barnes. The real Djuna Barnes is dead." She feels she must get many things done quickly, that she is running out of time. Everything is out of print and she wishes to remedy this; she urged me to keep trying to place *Ryder*. She says a group of people approached her in 1972 about placing the book with a publisher, but they were a group of "foolish, mawkish lesbians," and she refused their overtures even though they were recommended by friends. She is also considering giving the new animal poems to Ben Raeburn's Horizon Press if he will offer a modest advance.

A new character emerged towards the end of our visit: a six-foot-four-inch, piano-playing former fiancé named Putzi Hanfstaengl. She says he was Hitler's official pianist and wrote some German anthems in the 1920s. He was one of the people who helped hide Hitler after the Munich affair, and he told her she could interview him for two dollars a word, but no one wanted to pay the bill in those days. She says this is too bad; she could have met Hitler and then turned him in and where might that have led? Perhaps she'll talk about this Putzi and his friend, Hitler, at a later date.

3 November

The animal poems—A is for Alas—are in a pile of papers about three inches thick. We sorted them carefully today and seem to have the final two versions. There are about fifty pages of each letter, all mixed and jumbled together, but now there are two complete sets, in proper order, and Miss Barnes promises to tackle it this weekend.

She is interested in the poems; they are not marvelous but at least they are charming, and she wants them issued. She is in no great hurry, but this is probably a pose now that the project is underway. The latest draft, one of the two she is using, is dated April 1971. *Harpers* wanted to issue it some years ago, but only if it was properly illustrated. I made a good guess when I suggested drawings, but I did not do so well with Edward Gorey. She is certain he will not do. I told her he also illustrates children's books in a slightly less morbid fashion.

She is slightly hesitant about these animal verses. She wants to know if I like them. I tell her yes, they're charming. She wants to be coaxed so I coax her, and after a long conversation she finally says, "All right, I'll finish it for you." This is progress. If she works on these and they are accepted, which should not be a problem, perhaps it will spur her on to work on more serious material.

She saw a book of portraits by Richard Avedon sticking out of my bag and wanted to see it. She thinks it is dreadful. She knows (knew) some of the people in the book and is upset that he made them look so awful. Avedon photographed her in the 1950s; he sent a car to call for her, and the photographs were made in a studio. She is surprised she consented at the time and never saw the results; if they are like those in the book, she is glad she didn't and hopes they remain hidden from view forever. She does not think the portraits were ever published anywhere or she would have known about it.

More of what she enjoys best—writers. She once enjoyed William Faulkner very much, particularly *The Sound and the Fury*, but became bored with him. Antoine de St. Exupéry is charming but little more. James Thurber is wonderful; she likes him a great deal and loves his drawings. He once told her she was one of the few people he knew who had a real sense of humor. She dislikes Anais Nin both as a writer and personally. She used to see her walking around the Village but usually wouldn't speak to her. Nin's pornographic stories that were recently issued are simply terrible.

Incidentals: Miss Barnes was once offered a job as an editor at *Vanity Fair*, but she turned it down. It was not important because everyone was offered the job at least once and it paid only fifteen dollars a week.

Eliot once told her she is in *Finnegan's Wake*. She asked if he could recall the page, but he couldn't. She said she never looked for the entry, she'd be damned if she'd read the entire book for it.

In her opinion, "Quarry" is a very important work. The first line, "While I unwind duration from the tongue-tied tree," is one of her favorites. She explained about the rings in a tree, one for each year of her life, and how she was unwinding them in her mind during the course of the poem, or was unwinding them while writing the poem. If you don't know the meaning of "sowl," it is impossible to figure out the ending of the poem. She has made it complicated, but is distressed that so few people understand the meaning of it. To her it is very simple and to the point. Eliot used to tell her, "Miss Barnes, you are unique; there is no one like you."

As our conversation wound down she said that some people say in a few hundred years she may be as important as Shakespeare. She added that she doubted it and laughed loudly. She wonders why people think her work is morbid; she tries to inject as much humor into it as possible.

8 November

Miss Barnes is convinced that only two or three of the animal verses are worthwhile; there has not been as much progress as I had hoped. She feels the poem about the seal is adequate, but is concerned that by comparison with so many poems written by others about animals, hers will appear poor. She needs as much encouragement as possible. She is trying to keep her spirit up and not let all her physical problems get her down, but it must be difficult. Again, "Djuna Barnes is dead; the only thing I have left is my voice. I was born with a dominant voice and, asthmatic or not, it is still there." The real problem with the animal poems or anything else is that there may not be enough creative energy left to finish it. This is her primary worry and she talks of it constantly.

She feels she may not have the energy to finish even the most trivial verses, like those about seals, lions, and monkeys. At one point she looked at me and said, "Young man, do you feel like making love every day?" Some days, most days in fact, she does not feel like anything at all and has repeated for the hundreth time, "if you can't be marvelous. . . ." Then she quotes Eliot, "I have nothing to say and I'm saying it."

One reason she was uninterested in reissuing *Ryder* is that she feels it treats religion very lightly in the character of Dr. O'Connor. After the book was published she changed her mind and vowed never to mock religion, even in the most casual fashion, not because she is religious but because many people desperately need religion and there is no need to offend them. She is an agnostic; all she believes in is her own ignorance and does not know enough to know whether there is a supreme being or not. She is most emphatic about this.

On the lighter side, she once interviewed the heavyweight champion Jack Johnson, who pinched her bottom, and the other great champion Jack Dempsey, who didn't. The legendary Joe Gould was to her a dirty Village character who never wrote one sensible word and tagged along after e.e. cummings. She can't understand how cummings tolerated him. She spoke of the three men Berenice always refers to as her own surrogate fathers: Hippolyte Havel, Terry Carlin, and Sadakichi Hartmann. Havel was often found lying in the gutter, but his collar would be clean; Carlin lived to be 104; and Hartmann was the father of babies with everyone in sight and wanted to have one with her.

I had left the book of Atget's photographs with quotations from Marcel Proust, and she loved it. She never met either of these artists and profoundly regrets not having known Proust. She says Natalie

Barney did manage to have one late night meeting with him; Miss Barnes is very jealous about this. Proust arrived very late, bundled up against the cold, and Barney thought she was going to have a grand time telling him about all her sexual conquests, but apparently never managed to do so because Proust kept telling her of his. Barney had to wait for another day which never came. Miss Barnes feels it is best to read the later Proust and skip his first work; she thinks his early writing is just not first-rate.

It is a big jump from Proust to cockroaches, but this was her next subject. A fair number of roaches run about, under the bed and in the kitchen, and Miss Barnes is concerned about them. A roach bomb is out of the question, so I suggested the possibility of a "roach motel." She was horrified. A little box with glue under her bed? "A roach motel is much too personal; we can't have those horrid little creatures checking in and leaving their names, now can we?" I wish I had recorded this conversation.

12 November

We visited with another eye doctor today to get a second opinion: Dr. Harvey Lincoff at New York Hospital. It was a great effort for Miss Barnes to go out today. She was very fierce with the doctor, probably because she had to wait so long, and once she had an audience she made certain he listened to a great deal. She outlined all the different opinions she has heard over the years concerning her eyes. At the end of it the doctor suggested a slight modification of her glasses. The cash register at The Eye Shop must be listening. On the way back to Patchin Place she gave me more of her medical history. In addition to everything else she had told me, there was the operation for a double hernia, a broken arm, removal of part of her stomach for cancer, removal of part of her small intestine for diverticulitis, and a minor nervous breakdown in 1971. She must be made of iron to have survived all this.

I told Miss Barnes I planned to see a play by Noel Coward; she thinks he was "terrific" because he knew how to use language properly. He never attempted to write anything deep; he just wrote plays that were very good and entertaining. At some point he was thrown out of the Theater Guild, she says, because he was a "pansy," but she was away and had nothing to do with it. The people who threw him out regretted what they had done after he became so successful.

A few personalities came up from the distant past: Jack London, to whom she wrote a fan letter and he replied, and Maude Adams, who used to send her tickets to various plays, including *Peter Pan*.

The old worries about her poems are still there; she's not certain that any of the later ones are good enough to go in a book for general release, but she wants to keep working on them nonetheless. She hopes the new glasses will make it easier.

17 November

The new glasses are in hand, but her first reaction was not good. Finally, however, she gave them a try and is now reading without the magnifying glass. This may mean there is one less excuse for not working.

The University of Maryland has offered ten thousand dollars for all her miscellaneous papers and old bills. She feels it may not be proper to sell them. It is true that most are just business letters and accumulation, but she should sell them. If the university people want everything, why not let them have it? She has saved everything made of paper and is forever making notations on any scrap in sight, and then, once written on, saving it for future reference. Poems are on grocery lists, papers piled here and there in no apparent order. She says there are a good many decent poems buried in the piles of papers. I believe her, but it will take a mine detector to discover them.

The discovery will have to wait; we worked on the animal poems. She is now satisfied with the first six verses but does not want any to be printed unless they are up to the standards of the seal and the giraffe. She is having trouble with the letter "I." We went through various dictionaries looking for animals and unusual words with little success.

She told me she voted for Susan Sontag to become a member of the Academy; she feels sorry for her because she has been ill and is probably a decent person.

19 November

Miss Barnes is still working on the animals. The flying fish is revised and complete. She asked me to start sorting through the piles of papers while she played with her menagerie. I found some correspondence from T. S. Eliot she had been searching for. It included her remembrances of their last meeting (1965) when she knew he was very ill. This batch of papers is very important to her; Eliot's life was essentially over by then, and his last words to her were, "Goodbye, my darling." She never saw him again.

There are hundreds of poems lying scattered all about, dozens of versions of the same poem, long poems, short poems, complete and incomplete drafts all mixed together—some are edited, others are not. Boxes and piles and piles of unorganized papers. Perhaps I can make sense out of some of it so she can at least try to finish a portion of her work.

In sorting through all the papers I came upon deposit slips and correspondence from Peggy Guggenheim. One reason Miss Barnes has been able to survive all these years with no income is that Peggy Guggenheim has been helping her. There is no indication of exactly when it started or for how much, but three hundred dollars arrives every month like clockwork.

The writer for the day is Ezra Pound. She first met him in Paris on an assignment to interview him for Margaret Anderson's periodical, *The Little Review*. He helped Miss Barnes find an apartment, but she refused to take it when she discovered the people next door were practicing black magic. Years later she visited Pound when he was confined by the U.S. government at St. Elizabeth's Hospital in Washington, D.C. To her surprise he spoke to her about their first meeting in Paris, and she almost fell over. She never saw him again. I told her I didn't care for Pound. She suggested that I not bother with him, but I should read anything by a Russian named Ivan Aleksandrovich Goncharov and another writer who used the name Comte de Lautreamont. I probably will not; I don't have time to read the people I've heard of and enjoy, and I've never heard of these writers.

Today she was more optimistic than usual. She now believes she will live a little longer; she has survived the worst. The pain, however, is constant and even though her doctor says she'll live to be ninety-four, she doesn't want to unless she can work on her poetry.

24 November

Miss Barnes was not in very good shape when I arrived. She said she's feeling terrible because of the pain in her lower spine. She's tried to work on the animal poems but with no success at all. Some days it is impossible to have any ideas, let alone a marvelous one. She looks at *Nightwood* and wonders whatever gave her the inspiration to write it. We discussed inspiration; it is her opinion that normally we are incapable of grand things and when something exceptional happens, when we are truly inspired, we might not even be ourselves but someone else: an interesting idea. The conversation was a good deal more developed and complicated than this, but this summary touches the highlights.

In the middle of this conversation Allegra Kent, the ballerina, telephoned me; she was very upset, on the verge of utter despair. I was not good at hiding my concern. When she telephoned again, still not revealing where she was calling from, Miss Barnes began to share my concern. After I told her the bare outlines of the problem, she became even more concerned than I, all for a person she had never met and only knew of slightly, ballet not being one of her primary interests. She was genuinely worried and upset that we were both powerless to do anything; she has been there before, I suspect. When she said she understood the problem, it was probably because she had suffered similar depression and, recognizing it, transferred the futility of her own position, stuck in a small room and largely confined to bed. Miss Barnes looked at me sternly and said, "I've seen death and I didn't like it."

I stayed much longer than I'd planned; she wanted to talk and the more she talked, the more interesting and animated she became. As time passed she became even more excited and began to laugh a good deal. It is interesting to try and follow her thought processes; they often don't seem to make much sense. One minute she says, "I don't want to talk about all those terrible things going on in Guyana; I've had my fill of that. . . . Ezra really thought his early poems were very good when he did them. He was very sincere and the work meant a great deal to him." I don't think I'll ever figure how Jim Jones and his followers in Guyana led her to Ezra Pound.

There was once a reading of *The Antiphon*, she thinks, in Boston. The audience was T. S. Eliot, Edwin Muir, and herself. The reading was peculiar. "Tom Eliot was sitting on one side wiggling and Muir was on the other being very serious." She feels the reading went well enough until the last line was read improperly. Later, Herbert Berghof wanted to produce the play at his studio and sent a car to pick up Miss Barnes, so she might see the performance space and meet with various people who might be involved in the production. She went to the studio, took one look, and walked right out. She has heard a rumor that the play was once produced in Germany but has no proof. She wrote another play after *The Antiphon*, but tore it up because it was stylistically too close to the former drama, and she repeated: "It is very important not to repeat one's self." She also repeated her fear that the play may be pretentious and other fears concerning the translation.

Ryder caused problems with her family. Her mother threw the book out the window after she read it, and one of her brothers wouldn't speak to her after he became aware of its contents. He felt a proper lady should not write of such things. She also spoke of her father, who was stern but talented, accomplished in many disciplines; he could play the violin, write an opera or a novel, and run a farm. He could do anything he wanted to and was encouraged by his mother to try anything at all. Miss Barnes mentioned two other relatives, a half brother and a half sister, both living in Philadelphia, but she is not close to either of them. She is detached from all these relatives and recalled the time—sometime in the 1960s—she was in the hospital "dying," when two of her brothers came to call at the same time. They ignored her and spent most of the time arguing with one another over a lunch date one or the other had missed. What a family. She feels she is lucky to have survived that stay in the hospital; an intern told her they were experimenting on her.

Miss Barnes talked about the Baroness Elsa Von Freytag-Loringhoven, who kept mice as pets and a small dog locked away in her closet. The mice ran all over her bed; she fed them there and didn't think this behavior was in any way unusual.

She began to talk of her newspaper interviews. Miss Barnes once pursued the musical comedy star Fanny Brice, who was living with a gangster. The paper wanted the inside story but though Miss Barnes managed to get to Brice, the lady wouldn't talk. She is proud of having managed to corner the Duchess of Marlborough, who never saw *anyone*, but invited her to tea, and remembers asking whether the Duke had any interest in politics, whereupon everyone roared with laughter. One hilarious story followed another, some not so funny but described in a very amusing way. I told her so, and she replied, "Yes, they used to ask me to dinner simply because I was so amusing. I'm not so amusing anymore." I said this was not the case, that she should do a book of witty anecdotes. Her response? "I've been offered millions for my memoirs but always refused." I told her to keep telling me stories, and she did so into the night. Her spirit is amazing.

25 November

A very hurried visit. Miss Barnes likes James Thurber, so I took her a copy of *Further Fables for Our Time*—the type is large and it is full of animals. She wasted no time and began reading it without her magnifying glass. She likes Thurber even though he was unkind to women; he was equally unkind to his drawings, many of which E. B. White rescued from the wastebasket. She used to enjoy White because he wrote so well, but wonders why he is such a stickler for perfect grammar.

Newspaper days and interviews again. She finally quit the papers because of a rape case in which a girl in her teens had been raped six times. The editor of the *Journal American* wanted an interview with the victim and suggested that Miss Barnes contrive a story to gain access to the girl. She managed to sneak past the guards at the hospital, entered the girl's room, made up some wild tale, and got an interview, but when it was over felt guilty about what she had done. When she told her editor she would never cover another rape case and would not write a story about this one or give the information to anyone else, he fired her on the spot.

She also described her interview with the tough gangster, "Baby Face" Nelson, who lived on Waverly Place. His girlfriend was with him, and guards were at the door for the entire time. Another of her assignments was to interview the father of a girl who had been murdered. She went to his house, managed to get in, and saw the body in the living room, but when the outraged family threw her out, she went back into the house through an upstairs window and managed to take a photograph of the dead girl. This too is what made her get out of the newspaper business.

27–28 December

A good deal of contact over the past days and weeks, but mostly just simple conversation about the holidays and related matters. She returned the plum pudding, but kept the rest of the presents. She is finished with my copy of Guillaume Apollinaire's *Le Bestiaire*. It has encouraged her; she feels her animal verses are much better than Apollinaire's. The camel has been revised, it is now complete, and the lion is well underway. Time is her main problem. She feels capable of working one or two hours a day and finds it hard to concentrate for a longer period. She is, however, pleased with the results of the last month and spoke of a long poem she has been working on "for ten years or so." It is almost finished but considerably reduced.

A new concern of hers is the publication of a small book entitled *Greenwich Village As It Is*. The Phoenix Book Shop in New York has published it and sells it at a price of twenty dollars. She is unhappy about it, describing it as a simple article that appeared in a newspaper many years ago. The distress is caused by her belief that someone may read the book and think it represents her serious work. "I did it to pay the rent. It costs twenty dollars and you can buy *Nightwood* for seventeen dollars less. What kind of fool would pay twenty dollars for this silly little book?" As she threw it across the room she added, "This is worth about four cents!" I offered her a nickel for it, and my offer was accepted with a laugh. At the same time the people at the Phoenix are trying to be honorable; they sent her a six hundred dollar "royalty," but Miss Barnes is disinclined to accept it. After much arguing she finally agreed to accept the money. It will be used to pay a masseuse to work on her legs, which grow increasingly numb each day.

Today was a day to tear into people. She honestly feels everyone
will do you in for money and added, "Eliot even did," but stopped
and did not elaborate. The world is in a shabby state. She is sorry
about it and even sorrier to be living in Greenwich Village, which
has become increasingly dreadful. I think I convinced her it is still
a better place to live than many places in New York and gave her
some graphic examples. She was horrified.

Berenice Abbott asked Miss Barnes to write the text for *Greenwich Village Today and Yesterday*, but she refused. She had no
interest in the Village then, and does not now. She also mentioned
that the Baroness Elsa originally wanted to leave all her possessions
to Berenice, but they wound up with someone else, except for the
manuscripts and assorted poems and drawings. She makes every
effort to seem stern in discussing Berenice, but I think she does it
for effect.

Ignorance was the next topic. She repeated that she only believes
in her own ignorance. This is valid, I said, but it is clear that some
people possess a good deal more ignorance than others. She laughed
loudly and said this was my noble thought for the day. Then she
looked at me and said, very seriously, she was convinced she had
wasted her life until the day she told this to Eliot, who told her she
may have wasted some of it, but she should look very carefully at
what she had done when she was not wasting it.

She feels her life was least wasted in writing *Nightwood*: "I know
it is very, very good but at times I cannot understand how I could
have been good enough to have written it." She is concerned with
everything that happens to the book, what everyone thinks and
writes about it; she wants it to live at least forever. I told her I'd
reread it recently and she wanted to know everything I thought,
questioning me about the smallest details. She says the manuscript
was almost lost; she left it at the foot of her bed one night, a bed

covered with "handmade satin sheets, a comforter, and old religious vestments." The bed was close to a fireplace, and she woke to find the bedclothes burning; the fire was just reaching the manuscript. She snatched it out of the flames, then put out the fire. "If it had burned there would have been no *Nightwood*. I could never have written it again."

Dan Mahoney often told her she had ruined him because so many people came to him later, wanting to write down what he said. *Nightwood* was not written by simply taking down Mahoney's remarks; this is not the way it happened at all. She visited with him frequently and listened to him talk, but never wrote down what he said. She was often in trouble with some of her friends because of him; they didn't think she should spend so much time with a dirty person like Mahoney. She didn't care if he was dirty or not; he was interesting and did supply some key ideas in the book. She did elaborate on some of the things he said to her, but never used long portions of his dialogue.

The earlier conversation about the fire brought up another story, this time from many years earlier. She was at the house of a friend, Fitzie, and was sitting at a typewriter hard at work. A fire broke out, the firemen came and went, but she was so absorbed she never left the typewriter and didn't even stop typing until the fire had been extinguished.

31 December

I dropped in to see whether Miss Barnes needed anything to get through New Year's Eve or the following day. In good spirits but in ill health, she can't seem to eat anything. She wanted to talk, so I sat down. As I did she asked what kind of poetry I liked, and I confessed I didn't read very much poetry; it is not my favorite diversion. She laughed and said, "No one does! Why should you be any different?"

I told her I had an issue of *The New Republic* in my bag and that they often had poetry reviews; her interest was obvious. She said, "Well, let's have a look." I found a review written by Joyce Carol Oates of an anthology that had singled out two for discussion. I read them aloud to Miss Barnes. The first, "The Married Man" by Robert Phillips, was reviewed favorably. Miss Barnes asked what I thought, and innocently I said I didn't think it was a poem at all, but rather a short piece of prose cut up by the author to suit his fancy, lines cut willy nilly, just a bit of an idea that was an undeveloped piece of prose. She looked at me sternly and said, "Don't think you've discovered anything. That's all most of them do. It is NOT poetry. I could cut up *Nightwood* that way and it would be more of a poem, which, of course, it isn't."

The second poem, "Blackleaf Swamp" by Mary Oliver, never made it to the discussion stage. As I was reading it Miss Barnes had a coughing fit, so we stopped talking of poetry. When she caught her breath she wanted to talk about lighter subjects.

She brought up the subject of recording and said people have been after her to do it for years. She now feels she should have recorded when her voice was better. Her voice was once so good people begged her to go on the stage. She had no interest, but she did appear in two plays in the teens, in *The Tidings Brought to Mary* by Paul Claudel as a nun and in Leo Tolstoy's *The Power of Darkness*. She was terrified in both. There is a photograph of her in the Claudel play, on her knees praying.

She threw in one zinger, discussing her interview with Mrs. Warren G. Harding, the wife of the president. She said the woman was so frightfully dull it was no wonder her husband ran around.

The last topic was a sculpture of her, a bust, which her brother is finishing. He wishes to have it cast in bronze and given to the University of Maryland. She says it is a worthless piece of nonsense and she certainly doesn't want it around the house; it might fall on her, as did the deathmask of Baroness Elsa, which was once in her closet.

What about New Year's Eve? She hates New Year's Eve and hates parties in general. She hated them when she was young and hates them now—a complete waste of time. Happy New Year!

1–20 January 1979

I've had many short meetings with Miss Barnes. There has been some progress. She has completed more of the animal poems and continues to work on them. More importantly, St. Martin's Press has offered a three thousand dollar advance to publish *Ryder*. She wants the opinion of a third party about whether this is a fair offer and asked Robert Beare at the University of Maryland, who told her to accept it. Now all that is needed is a contract and a copy of the previous edition that St. Martin's can cut up. She has seen the standard St. Martin's contract and says it will not do; most of it doesn't apply to *Ryder*. I don't blame her; most of it is complicated legal nonsense. I asked if she wants a fine edition of *Ryder*, a limited edition with a photograph of herself by Berenice, and she made it very clear she does not want it to be a joint effort with Berenice Abbott.

The bank account is increasing; a small bequest from Janet Flanner is in hand, and she has accepted the six hundred dollars from the Phoenix Book Shop for the tiny Greenwich Village book. She continues to be upset with it as well as with another publication—*Unmuzzled Ox*—for reprinting some of her newspaper interviews. She is certain the University of Maryland is supplying all these people who are issuing unauthorized editions. She is also concerned about Andrew Field, who is writing a biography of her, but realizes she can do nothing to stop him. She is even more upset with a niece whom she thinks is snooping around the library in Maryland, going through her papers, trying to come up with enough scandal and information to do a book. All she wants is to be free from people prying into her affairs, to have enough strength to work at her poetry, and live to see a handsome edition of *Nightwood* issued. The paperback edition now in print is inadequate, and the hardcover edition, issued some years ago by New Directions, is not sufficient.

She is eating badly and fell the other day. There is a constant worry that she may fall and be unable to get up. She says it takes all her strength just to talk to someone on the rare occasion that there is anyone to talk with, and she keeps her nitroglycerin pills close at hand.

21 January

Miss Barnes telephoned me very early this morning and with a sense of urgency said she feels terrible and her days are numbered. There are many things that need to be handled in an orderly fashion. I went over later in the day.

She's had a premonition that everything will be over by May or June, and there is much she wishes to accomplish. The first order of business is the Baroness Elsa Von Freytag-Loringhoven. It is urgent that someone do something sensible with her poetry and letters.

She wants me to make certain they are published, and the first step is for her to write a letter to the "authorities" at the University of Maryland authorizing me to go through all of Baroness Elsa's papers and make copies. It is unclear why Miss Barnes retains all literary rights to these papers, but she maintains this is the case. In the late 1960s or early 1970s someone tried to work on them, but the worker in question turned out to be alcoholic, and the project was abandoned. Miss Barnes even tried to work on them many years before but also quit before anything was completed. She seems pleased that I will look at the papers and try to make some sense of them; she has even consented to recall, for the record, as much about the Baroness Elsa as possible. A secondary matter in all this is her concern about Berenice's reaction to publishing the material. Berenice was very close to the Baroness, and her letters are mixed in with all the other letters and manuscripts. She doesn't want to offend anyone, particularly Berenice. There were some problems between the three parties that will probably appear inconsequential in 1979 but were of great concern in 1927. I said the only things I care about are whether Baroness Elsa's poems are good (Miss Barnes claims they are) and whether there are enough good ones to make a sensible book (she says there are plenty).

The other matter of major concern is to finish up a few poems, be done with them, and destroy all the rough drafts. She knows someone will grab them when she dies and some fool will attempt to publish scraps of this and that. She is terrified (not a sufficiently strong word) of this happening, but can't gather the courage to throw anything away and is unable to see well enough, despite all the new glasses, to get anything in proper order. I told her she had to make the decision to finish some of the poems, or at least select the best versions, and discard all the drafts and various revisions. If she wants I will come by a couple of hours a day as regularly as possible and assist her in making some order out of the current chaos. I added that she will probably be remembered for *Nightwood*, *The Antiphon*, a few stories, and possibly whatever poems she might have managed to complete in these last few months or years. I wish I knew a little more about poetry.

She is very apprehensive about getting her poetry in order. Just as I started to leave she looked at the desk and then at me, saying, "This table is all that has kept me alive, and they want to take it away from me." She'll never forget how the people came in and piled her books and papers into boxes and hauled them off to the university.

22–27 January

This has been a very hard week of sorting poems. There is a rush because one of the doctors wants to operate and Miss Barnes will be incapacitated for a while. She is also upset with the University of Maryland because a book of her early stories is coming out and she's certain they are in league with the publishers, who she feels will also issue a book of her early plays, some of which are merely sketches and drafts. She does not want anyone to have access to the drafts of her poems, to work them over at a later date however they might like. All this left her in such a state of anxiety that she refused to see Robert Beare on 26 January.

The plan is to finish as many poems as possible and then burn all the remaining drafts. There are well over forty poems, long and short, in various stages. Some are complete, others are confusing drafts. All the different poems had been sorted into individual folders by 26 January, and the following day Miss Barnes worked hard on the one that begins, "Man cannot purge his body of its theme." We began at 4:00 and worked until midnight; she was up for it and feels she made great progress on this poem, which she thinks is the most important one she has ever attempted. There are at least five hundred drafts of this poem and many different titles. The most common are "Phantom Spring," "Viaticum," and "Rites of Passage." A variation of this last title will probably be selected. It has also been condensed and is now contained on a single sheet of legal-sized paper. The longer, unedited poems have such titles as "Derelictions," "Rakehill," "The Ponder Rose," "Tom Fool," and "The Laughing Lamentations of Dan Corbeau (The Book of Dan)." There are many others, some of which appear complete. I'm no expert, but some of the short poems are extremely interesting. There is one very long poem, about two inches of manuscript, entitled *Virgin Spring*. It will be a challenge to see if anything can be done with it.

She was misleading when she claimed she did not remember one line of poetry. She remembers many of the poems in her head. Give her a line and she can finish it. She is also fond of John Donne and enjoys using his ideas in her work. One of the short poems is dedicated to Eliot's wife, Valerie. I mentioned I had been looking at a facsimile edition of the typescript of *The Waste Land*, and she said she had seen it as well, adding she does not like the poem very much and "neither did his wife."

At one point I reached for a dictionary and next to it was *What 291 Means to Me*, the issue of *Camera Work* with the tributes. It was inscribed to "Djuna Barnes" from "The Old Man At 291" (the address of Alfred Stieglitz's gallery on Fifth Avenue). I asked how she obtained it. She used to go to the gallery and look at pictures and once showed some of her own work to Stieglitz. He hated the drawings but liked the artist and asked her to contribute to the issue, which she did. I asked what she thought about Stieglitz, and she had no opinion of him at all other than to say he wasn't decent to O'Keeffe sexually. She had absolutely no idea he took photographs but does recall one of her sitting on a couch at his gallery. She doesn't recall who took it and asked if his photographs are any good. I replied he made some good ones, but in my opinion he is vastly overrated.

The poems I have been sorting are very religious in a mysterious, non-secular fashion. I mentioned this and she said she is "rarely consciously religious, except with the mysteries of life and death and what everything means, if life means anything at all." These themes fascinate her. A profound hatred of her family is also obvious. Her father is the primary source of evil in the family; she shows more affection for her mother but dislikes her as well. We talked about this for some while, but the conversation drifted to her hatred of mushy women, intolerance of lesbians, particularly those who bother her about it, and a general intolerance for the sexually indulgent. "You will find it is better to write one good line than to make love all night!"

Her tolerance level is low; the poems often display a disparaging attitude toward men. One poem is about castration and another begins by speaking of the famine of a kiss from an old man's mouth. Yet, there is also an affectionate poem about the need for a special park for old men to "piddle in." The papers are turning up many interesting items. There are two three-act plays that are complete, but the acts are divided between Miss Barnes and the university. The main character in one is Jane Barkman. *An Irish Triangle* was written under the influence of J. M. Synge; she now feels Synge is not very good and is certain her play was terrible when it was written and even worse now. She is working vigorously and desperately wants to finish her poems, trying all the while to make certain each and every line is marvelous. I hope she can manage.

At my urging she signed the Andrew Field contract. It stipulates a payment of one thousand dollars to use quotations from her work in his book, up to 5 percent of the total number of words in the manuscript. She made an interesting point; by the stipulations in the contract, if Field's book contains enough words, he might very well use every word she has ever written. I said it was an amusing point, but I'd be surprised if it turned out that long, so she might as well take the money. She can use it; he can quote anyway, and it is far better to have Field as a friend than an enemy.

29 January–3 February

This was a very good week with Miss Barnes. We worked at least three hours every day on the poetry, sometimes even longer. All the papers have now been sorted a second time, with many missing or misplaced manuscript pages being found. It seems there are forty or fifty completed poems that just need a little work, so it may be possible to assemble a good, though modest book. She has settled on two titles: *The Rites of Spring* for the major poem and *Figures in an Alphabet* for the animal verses. The plan is to tidy these two poems and then work on the rest. If she can manage this, she plans to attack "Laughing Lamentation" and "Satires." The work is very slow, but she is making steady progress each day.

The illustrations for *Ryder* are now in order and she has selected one for the cover. The back of the dust jacket will feature the Man Ray portrait. I've written a short forward that gives a brief history of the book, and Lee Witkin, the noted photograph gallery owner, is interested in a show of the drawings. Miss Barnes is pleased with all this progress.

The amusing stories keep pouring out. It's unfortunate that she doesn't wish to be recorded. It almost seems she is making up for lost time; she hasn't talked with anyone for so long and now that the opportunity exists, she is unable to stop, at one point saying, "I wish you knew more about some of these people. Then you'd know more about what I'm telling you." She loves to tell a story, make a sarcastic remark, and then laugh along with me. She said, "Henry James was a silly pansy," then adds, after the briefest pause, "but he didn't work at it." Roaring laughter. It seems almost all the men she knew were, as she calls them, "pansies," and she speaks of this aspect of their character condescendingly. Most of her female associates were lesbians, but she is less harsh with them, except for those who attempted to bed her. She laughs at those ladies because most of them failed. In discussing these people she can be very tender and then harsh, barely drawing a breath between statements. On Robert McAlmon: "He was the saddest man I ever knew because he wasn't Joyce and wanted to be so badly." Within a second he became Robert McAlimony because the woman he married was as gay as he and all he wanted was access to her family's money. Then back to McAlmon selling copies of *Ladies Almanack* and his having "every right to do so since he paid for it."

She made two passing comments, one about Natalie Barney, the other about Gurdjieff. She doesn't take either person seriously. She said it's true, Evangeline Musset in *Ladies Almanack* is Barney, but she "never gave her permission to say she was and she said it all the time." She met Gurdjieff and quickly discovered he was an old fraud, a man "of the opinion he could completely cure you of anything by simply looking at you, but he never chose to look."

"IN MY CASE IT HAS ONLY BEEN PAINFUL AND NASTY."

Miss Barnes is annoyed that I know so little about poetry. She is forever asking what I think about this line or that, and all I can do is offer a spontaneous reaction. She says: "None of it is easy and even little throwaway lines are very difficult. Each word must be carefully crafted and it is the hardest kind of writing." Speaking of some things that pass as poetry in 1979, she said, "If that stuff is poetry, I'll eat the flour."

*Barnes,
London
circa
1935*

I had known Barnes slightly more than four months, but our relationship was slowly evolving into something markedly differ-ent from anything I had anticipated. It was unclear why she wished to see me so frequently, particularly since she had chosen to remain isolated and aloof for so many years. It may have been that she was desperate, or perhaps we simply hit it off and enjoyed talking with one another. Nonetheless, by early February things were starting to change, changes that were not reflected in the diary entries.

Barnes was working more, and I was spending more time away from my recording studio/record production business to drop in and chat, tend to whatever mail may have come in, and to see how much work she was accomplishing. All this extra activity led to an early morning telephone call on 4 February. I was in my private editing room when an assistant knocked on the door; Barnes was on the line, which was unusual for she rarely got up before noon. Except for the days when I took her to visit her many doctors, I had never seen her earlier than mid-afternoon. She was very upset and almost pleaded with me to drop whatever I was doing and come over to her apartment as quickly as possible. There was such a sense of urgency in her voice that I left an unedited master tape on the recorder and hurried over to Patchin Place. Within the hour I was sitting behind her desk as she explained what she felt was such an urgent matter.

The night before had been dreadful; she thought she was going to die and was terrified because none of her affairs were in proper order. Her days were numbered; she was convinced she had less than six months to live and wanted to organize her affairs as well as possible. She had selected me to assist her actively in the process. She added firmly that I was "not her husband or a relative" and she wished to pay me for my services. I replied in an equally firm manner that what I had done for her up to then had been done because it suited my pleasure, that she didn't have enough money to pay me on an hourly basis, and that even if she did I wouldn't accept it. I explained as tactfully as possible that I had stopped working for a "salary" some years earlier and my time was not for sale. I made it clear I was willing to help her get her affairs in order; in fact, I was already doing so, but under no circumstances would I accept any payment. My attitude surprised her; I remember her saying, "but everybody needs money," and my replying that was true, but she needed what little she had far more than I. She was somewhat shaken by this encounter; not expecting it to end this way, she said she would have to rethink my assisting her because she felt it would be less than honorable if she didn't compensate me for all the work she had in mind. The sense of urgency passed. We talked about less serious matters, and I returned to my studio to work on the master tape I had abandoned earlier.

The following day Barnes telephoned again, this time in the afternoon, and asked me to come by whenever it was convenient. Her attitude had changed and when we met later that afternoon it was apparent from the outset that she had been seriously reconsidering her position. She said she had a new idea, one that might satisfy both our needs. It was a simple proposal: I would assist her with all her business affairs, primarily looking after copyrights and reissues, arrange for better rates for her money, deal with lawyers and doctors, and see to all her correspondence not of a personal nature. In return she planned to "remember me in her will" and to name me executor of her estate. In this way I would not be taking any money she might need, but she would know I might eventually be compensated. I thought about her offer for about five seconds and agreed to her conditions; I was already doing everything she wanted and had never been an executor. The proposed arrangement, I thought, might be as challenging as it was interesting: for example, simple matters, like arranging book contracts around the world. Barnes's books had a modest U.S. and international following, but as I had become more familiar with all her published work I had become increasingly convinced it should all stay in print as long as possible in every country where there might be interest.

It was fairly obvious why Barnes chose me for this particular assignment. I was in the right place at the right time and highly recommended by an old friend of hers. There was no one else in her life at the time who could have done the job or had the ability or disposition to do what needed to be done. My disposition was far more significant than my ability. I was not a lesbian, was not a collector of poets, did not think *Nightwood* was the finest piece of prose penned in the twentieth century, and was in no particular awe of Barnes as a towering literary figure. I was not emotionally tied to her writings, her mystique, or Barnes herself. To me she was an extraordinarily bright woman who lived in a time warp, governed by values which she regarded as universal but which in fact stopped on the other side of her front door.

This was interesting to me, yet there was another equally fascinating aspect. Barnes was unique in my eyes because she was so innately intelligent, proper, and disinclined to gossip that she was an ideal person with whom to discuss the most sensitive of matters. I knew nothing would leave her room, and her opinions were not influenced by any trendy considerations. She was bound by a peculiar Old Testament/Ten Commandment morality jumbled with a mixture of Victorian propriety and Anglican piety that often provided a unique or at least novel approach to contemporary problems. We disagreed on many matters; some of her opinions seemed strange to me, but she knew that while I might disagree with her, I nonetheless respected her very much. For the most part she treated me in the same fashion. I wasn't a poet, but Barnes was impressed with my efficiency. She marveled at how I could sit at a typewriter and dash off a business letter without mistakes or understand a contract with a single reading. She commented on this frequently and when she did, I usually replied I was equally astonished with the way she could use words I could uncover in her collection of ancient dictionaries. We were at an intellectual stand-off, had a good understanding and working relationship, enjoyed one another's company, and realized there was much work we had to accomplish. This arrangement operated smoothly for about two years and then it suddenly deteriorated.

In Barnes's mind the first matter of business was to get her will in proper order because she was convinced she might die at any moment. This was ultimately an easy affair, but there were a number of interesting twists along the way. It began with Barnes providing me with the name of her lawyer, Mr. Osmond K. Fraenkel. He was with a Wall Street firm, Hays, St. John, and she suggested I call on him. I made an appointment and met with him later the same week. I was surprised to find that Mr. Fraenkel was even older than Barnes—well over ninety—but in his office every day. I found out he was a legendary figure in the field of civil rights, with an impressive record dating back to the 1920s. I was over-whelmed with this vigorous ninety-year-old and impressed with his early advocacy of causes that were surely unpopular at the time. He was so elderly, however, that I hesitated to suggest he visit with Barnes at home; he was, after all, six years older. But he insisted. He said he "lived around the corner" and could stop by on his way to work. I reported all this to a disbelieving Barnes. She was not even certain he was still alive when she suggested I call him, but a few days later Mr. Fraenkel appeared at Barnes's door. They had a fine discussion, and an assistant carefully noted the points Barnes wanted covered in her will. I learned at this point the executor I was replacing was Mr. Fraenkel's daughter.

Barnes,

1933

$\mathcal{A}$s outlined and eventually drawn, Barnes's requirements were simple: there were a few minor monetary requests, all her U.S. copyrights were to be given to the Author's League (she was very fond of the then-Executive Director, Peter Hegge), all European copyrights were left to St. Bride's of Fleet Street (it had taken a good deal of searching to find the appropriate Christopher

Wren-designed church), and any remaining money in her estate was to be equally divided between the Author's League, St. Bride's, and myself. I was to be executor of the estate, her remains were to be scattered on Storm King Mountain, and, most importantly, I was charged with burning all existing notebooks, manuscripts, drafts of poems, and miscellaneous papers that Barnes had not personally approved for publication. In her mind, this final provision was the most important. She didn't want anyone pawing through her rough notes and poems once she was dead, and a week never passed when she didn't remind me of this duty.

She found it impossible to burn her own papers, particularly the older ones, but on occasion I would arrive and find her at the fireplace burning current, inadequate drafts. It was a matter of great concern to her and she constantly chided me, saying I'd never burn them, but I always assured her I would and, in fact, had every intention of doing so. There are far too many examples of sloppy writers assembling minor works from the notes of significant authors. I hoped at the time it would be possible to work out one acceptable, small volume of poems that met with her approval before it was necessary to destroy sixty-five years of her notebooks and assorted writings.

At some point in the next weeks Osmond Fraenkel and his assistant returned with the will, properly executed. It became the most important document in Barnes's possession. She kept it within reach of her bed at all times, carried it in her purse when she visited the doctor, and took it with her when she checked into a hospital. On one visit to Lenox Hill Hospital there was a moment of uncertainty when the staff would not let her check in unless she placed her valuables and papers in the hospital safe. After some discussion this was arranged, but she kept inquiring about her will all the time she was hospitalized.

I was performing all the tasks she required and had been doing so for some time. I was, for all practical purposes, running many aspects of Barnes's life. As time passed it became necessary to take on more and more responsibilities, and while there were many problems I failed to anticipate, we managed to accomplish a good deal in the next twenty-seven months.

We "officially" began our structured relationship in March 1979. I gave up a little of my time and Barnes surrendered some of her stubbornly held independence. Little changed outwardly; I remained "Mr. O'Neal" and she was still "Miss Barnes." Throughout the entire time we worked together, we never addressed one another in any other way. In my absence she was not so formal; she used "Hank" in conversations with others, but never with me. Barnes preferred to be very formal, treated everyone she encountered in a proper, sometimes haughty fashion, and expected everyone to address her in a way befitting her stature and reputation. This shroud of formality was merely part of the mystery she consciously cultivated, and woe to anyone who happened to address her as Djuna. I witnessed it twice, once when a young woman presumed to call her by her given name and a second time with a noted doctor. It took the young lady months to regain access to Barnes. The doctor was another matter.

In mid-1979 Dr. Robert S. Coles implanted an artificial lens in one of her eyes. It was a daring move; Barnes's age prevented others from even considering an operation, but Coles felt she was a tough lady, and he was proven right when the operation was successful. It did give a slight amount of flexibility to an eye that was almost useless. A few weeks after she was discharged from the hospital, an office visit was scheduled to enable Dr. Coles to check her progress. The excursion uptown required great preparation on Barnes's part and my own, but we finally arrived. We had to wait a long time, but after more than an hour of fidgeting in the waiting room we were ushered into Dr. Coles's office. Barnes was very upset by the long wait; she was tired and cranky, outraged at what she perceived as bad manners. Suddenly, the doctor burst into the room, gave Barnes a hearty pat on the back, and said, "Well, how are you today, Djuna baby?" Barnes was rigid with disbelief, too stunned to reply. I doubt if anyone in the previous fifty years had ever addressed her so casually and given her a pat on the back for good measure. She was speechless, reduced to offering Dr. Coles a malevolent glare, primarily using the eye he had so recently repaired. She never stopped talking of his "impudence" and it probably nagged her to her dying day. She never visited him again, but the experience was not a total loss; an assistant in his office has been my doctor ever since.

The maintenance of the mystery of Djuna Barnes was crucial to her existence, as was the carefully controlled aura she had created for herself. She had done it for years and with time it became easier for her to maintain it; there was no one alive who knew enough to offer any meaningful contradiction. She had gone to great pains to preserve a mysterious fortress inside her tiny room, but as time went by, chinks fell out of the walls she'd created. Once one "secret" became known, many of the rest emerged and she became less complicated to understand. In fact, it was fairly simple, and over the next two years I learned why I was Mr. O'Neal, why Dr. Coles was impudent, and much more.

* * *

Barnes's immediate priorities, in my opinion—and my ideas were essentially the same as hers because the needs were so obvious—were to enable her to continue writing at some level, to prevent deterioration of her already fragile health, and to organize her literary and business affairs reasonably. We both understood if the latter two came under control, then the writing might at least become a possibility.

It was necessary to organize everything so as to prevent the slightest distraction from her writing. It may sound ludicrous but the preparation of a grocery list could easily become a four hour affair; it had to be typed, edited, revised, and finally telephoned to Jefferson Market. It was written just like a poem. Each began "Djuna Barnes, 5 Patchin Place, 2F, CH3-8134," all underlined in red, followed by the list of items. If an idea for a poem occurred after a notation for asparagus she would simply write it in and then proceed with ice cream and oranges. This led to confusing grocery lists needing extensive editing and revisions. It also led to saving all the grocery lists.

After the final version was called in to the market, there came the often interminable wait for the delivery boy who, if he brought only three cans of salt-free tomato juice instead of four, would be verbally abused, which he couldn't understand because he didn't speak English. He was also deprived of his twenty-five-cent tip as well, which he did understand, resulting in a few choice words in Spanish that Barnes never understood. If the order was faulty in any way—which, given the vagaries of grocery stores and Barnes's peculiar lists, was usually the case—it was enough to set her off for hours. Since almost everything she required had to be delivered by hand—food, medicine, laundry, whatever—there were usually

Jefferson,-675-2277. Nov 20.

qt Milk.

Half pound smelts.

[Of that balanced beast,the Unicorn.)

Abused by too much love;)   PRAISE

                              first
When he first fell into his mothers lake
                         ladies

That^ pool where human faces xayx come

and go)

C.O.Bigelow.   Gr. 7- 9200 .
             ——— ——

Dec10¢.0980

I Natracan.

Large (Mint) Milk of Magnesia.

(crenelated roof,holes for shooting through.)
 (Kyrie eleøison.-Lord have mercy.)
             ——

that stigeon pond,-lake.   **675**

Jefferson Market,Barnes.   Phone ~~857~~-2277

Qt.Milk.

~~Half pound of smelts~~

Half pound Port Salut.

6 oranges.

2 large kleenex.

one Kellogs No I9,wheat flakes?
✓ large BRILLO -- I--

Marmalade/Dundee..English.

~~Garlic (Clove)~~
~~Garlic...head of.~~

~~Kellogs wheat flakes No I9~~
~~Kellogs wheat flakes No I9.~~

Head of Garlic.   (damn.)   (clove)
Pure maple syrup.

2 Yogurt.   plain.

/ quarter pound Port-Salut cheese.

One Buitoni grated ~~cheese~~...parmison 3 ounces

liquid soap ?(Bald-headed man) Mr.Clean? Pint?

3 Haagen-Dazs Coffee ice cream (pints)

2 Cranapple   quarts

2 Sun-sweet prune juice 2 quarts

3 Malted milk ,natural . carnation

Half pound smelts. (3 Smelts.?)

1 Stella Doro bread sticks .

3 macintosh apples

constant opportunities for anger. When this happened, the "Oh, poor Miss Barnes" syndrome occurred: first anger, then resignation and back to bed.

Fretting over a can of tomato juice or the wrong brand of dental adhesive from Bigelow's Pharmacy was simply an excuse to be distracted and not get on with the poems, which had consumed the past forty years of her life, poems that meant much to her. The mind games she was playing were obvious. It was my job to eliminate the distractions and convince her they were inconsequential, and that it was cowardly to use the lack of a bottle of the proper brand of ginger ale as an excuse for not working.

It was often best to deal with certain situations lightly. The hours of preparation of grocery lists had to be stopped. I once suggested that her grocery lists were better than many people's poems and that she should consider publishing them. After all, she was saving them because of a good line or two; maybe it would be best to gather them all up, offer them to a publisher, and not only make some money but clear her desk as well. She looked at me sternly and then laughed; at least for a short while she spent less time worrying about the grocery lists.

Her health was another matter. She was very frail; her pain was real and almost constant. It was much easier to deal with the grocery lists and delivery boys than her myriad infirmities but, fortunately, she was much more tolerant of her physical condition than the failings of a grocery clerk. She complained about her various aches, pains, and lack of energy but endured them bravely. It was clearly impossible to stop the pain, short of addictive drugs, but it was a comparatively easy matter to attend to her eyes, lack of teeth, breathing difficulties, and relations with doctors and pharmacists.

General business, publishing, contracts, copyrights, and assorted paperwork were not complicated. The difficulties were usually created by Barnes herself. She procrastinated, held onto manuscripts, and was loathe to make decisions about publishing a new work or reissuing an old one. I had overcome the first reissue hurdle with *Ryder*; she agreed to get it back into print, worked with me on a brief introduction to put it in perspective, and consented to add some of the drawings that had been eliminated from the 1928 edition. The two additional drawings, mild by 1979 standards, must have shocked her editors fifty years earlier. She was happy to include them in the new edition, but decided to withhold a third that she considered distasteful. She felt it was acceptable to reproduce two of the expurgated drawings: one of a male angel flying through the air with a feather in his ass, peeking up the dress of a female angel, and another of the mother of the character Kate-Careless relieving herself in the street. She did not want to include a charming drawing of two old ladies knitting cod-pieces before a roaring fire. She would not even consider restoring the censored 1928 text. Her concern over the text had nothing to do with the words; she felt it would take too much time to restore all the excised expletives.

The reissue of *Ryder* brought a three thousand dollar advance; it proved to Barnes that it was possible to make modest sums from her old work with little effort. Once the first book was in the works, the reissues became a major project: I was determined to get everything back into print in every possible market. It was not a difficult task, and though Barnes treated each new contract as a bother, it pleased her that publishers the world over wanted to reissue her books. Also, she was pleased with the advances. She would often hold on to the checks for a week or two; it was fun just to have them in her purse. Once she had looked at them for a period of time she'd hand them over to me for deposit into one of her four savings accounts. The activity of reissuing books, watching bank accounts grow, not being forced to bother with any of it—just watching it happen—excited her and led to increased activity. I told her the entire process was easy because it *was* easy, and she expressed amazement. I eventually prepared a large chart that listed all her works and all the countries where it might be possible to license them. We then filled in the blanks. We would go over the progress we were making; a glance indicated progress in Spain, Italy, France, or other markets, and we managed to get almost everything back into print in every major Western European country.

She had started some work at the end of 1978, but with the schedule and knowledge that matters were under control, her work improved significantly. So did her conversations with me. The more she worked the more inquisitive she became. The more she talked the more there were things she wanted me to remember and, I felt, perhaps pass on to others. It is one thing to mention a matter casually in passing; it is something else to look at someone and sternly state a fact, and then, over the next two years, repeat it twenty or thirty times. There was much Barnes obviously hid from me and everyone else. Yet, there was much she did not hide, matters one would think she *would* have, particularly given her disposition and penchant for privacy. It was not the gossip and wild tales that were so revealing but rather the simple remark that often told most about her. Once she said, "The wish to be good is the wish to be destroyed." I don't know whether the statement was her own, but regardless of its authorship it guided her life. So she described hundreds of times how that particular virtue of hers had been her undoing.

One day she looked at me and said, "I always thought if I did anything wrong, if I took a pencil that didn't belong to me, if I was dishonorable in any way, in any fashion, then I would be unable to write a word. This is obviously not the case with others but I felt it was true for me." She did not say this casually or in an offhand way. She looked at me sternly as she said it; she wanted me to remember it and she repeated this frequently. The conversation returned to the virtue of Djuna Barnes at least once a week. Did she feel she was virtuous and thus destroyed or did she feel she had been dishonorable at some point and consequently unable to write? There was always the possibility she said such things to appear mysterious, but the fact remained that she had "retired" to one room in Patchin Place in 1940 and in the next forty years managed to publish one story, two short poems, and a play—given her talent, an inconsequential amount. Why was her output so small? Was it the result of some terrible circumstance? I thought the answer might be revealed in future conversations. As she was beginning to work so vigorously I thought there was a possibility that she had reconsidered and temporarily changed her beliefs— suppositions, unfortunately, that proved to be inaccurate.

Paris, 1925. This photograph was previously attributed to Man Ray; but later disclaimed by Juliet Man Ray.

The first order of business was to work on the poems. In fact, it was the only order of business. There were thousands of lonely, shut-in, eccentric elderly people in New York City and all of them probably needed assistance on some level. If I was to spend hours assisting one particular person in this category, I sincerely hoped something more than interesting conversations might result. This richly talented woman should finish some of her work. It was also a significant challenge; it would be wonderful if ninety-year-old Djuna Barnes issued a book of serious poems. It would add some polish to her reputation, shock a few critics, and amaze the handful of readers of serious poetry. She often stated she felt she retained the capacity to amaze, and I told her this was a way to prove it. I knew it would be very nearly impossible to accomplish anything particularly grand. Barnes once said to me, "I don't know if I should try and finish my poetry, burn all my papers, or lie in bed and scream!" She was doing all these things regularly, but I wanted to shift her emphasis to the poems.

For only three months I had been sifting through boxes, folders, and haphazard piles of papers that represented forty-plus years of her poetry output. While organizing it I read as many of her drafts as possible. I was not a poetry specialist (then or now) but her basic themes were apparent. It was not difficult to see what general ideas she was trying to develop. Why she was so overwhelmed with all the paper lying about her cluttered apartment was clear. It would have been difficult to sort with perfect vision. In her condition it was impossible. I attempted to make her understand that merely because she did not have the ability to keep her papers in sensible order in no way reflected on what she might be able to create if there was a modest amount of organization. I realized that the sheer bulk of the material would take a couple of lifetimes to organize, so I attempted to focus her on a few poems. Perhaps it was possible to bring those in the most finished state to a final version.

There were some obvious choices. I thought it would be a simple matter for her to clean up the animal poems she had been working on for many years. To encourage this I bought her bestiaries that had been done by others and books on obscure animals and legendary creatures. I found old books with drawings possibly more suitable in her eyes than those by Edward Gorey. While she looked at these books and pondered the fate of the animals in her final list, I continued to organize the rest of the poetry.

The drafts confirmed what I had suspected. While she was exceptionally clever and revealed a keen mind in conversation, she was narrow in her outlook, one of the most pessimistic and morbid writers I had ever encountered. Some of her early work was very witty, but the poetry that had occupied her for so many years, and much of her early work as well, was overflowing with death, grief, unfulfilled love, an overwhelming sense of doom, a pessimistic view of all of humanity. Most of it was couched in a gruesome, peculiar religiosity. I soon understood why she often said, "You may find me witty early in the evening but you'll hang yourself by morning." If she had left a rope next to some of the drafts, she might have been accused as an accessory to a suicide; it was difficult to be cheerful after reading page after page of her work, as she beat a few general themes to death.

I suspected that a good deal of Barnes's work from the 1940s and 1950s, and possibly later, was already filed at the McKeldin Library at the University of Maryland. Except for some large notebooks and a few miscellaneous items, almost everything that remained in her apartment was poetry. She once said, "They just came in and piled everything into barrels. It was all I could do to keep these few pages I have here to work with." She often characterized the day when her papers were removed as traumatic, with her tearing folders and assorted items from the hands of whoever was in charge of the removal. Much remained, however, and aside from the notebooks stored away in her large closet, the remaining papers indicated at one point that Barnes was writing a lengthy poem, variously titled *The Book of Dan*, *Laughing Lamentations*, *The*

Laughing Lamentations of Dan Corbeau, Virgin Spring, Derelictions, Of Derelictions, Parthenogenesis and Phantom Spring, or *Phantom Spring*. Some of the manuscripts were in the form of dialogue; perhaps these were remnants of the play she had written after *The Antiphon*, which she told me she had destroyed.

The more I read these assorted papers the more puzzled I became. It was apparent that even though there were various drafts, with different titles, as years had gone by the ideas of one poem had often been incorporated into others, and it was not unusual to see a line from one in a variety of different settings. It was almost as if the line was what was most important for her: strike a good line and then find a place to use it. The overall poem was secondary to one well-crafted line. In other instances entire sections would be transferred back and forth; but it appeared that all these drafts, mixed up and confusing though they seemed to be, were all part of a single poem of epic proportions.

I noticed this first by accident. I was familiar with Barnes's two poems published in *The New Yorker*, "Quarry" (1969) and "The Walking Mort" (1971). I hadn't originally read them in that magazine, but came upon them in Louis Kannestine's *The Art of Djuna Barnes—Duality and Damnation*. The ideas, single lines, and long sections of each poem were to be found in other longer, more elaborate verses created many years earlier. As I went through more and more papers I came upon the same situation time and time again. It was not unusual to find the same poem with any number of titles or the same title for any number of poems. In some instances the same poem would be written over a period of five years, where many drafts existed. The corrections on all the drafts would be the same. In other instances a poem with the same general idea and meter would have different words, and there were examples where lines would be reversed from one draft to another, or switched from one to another. In some cases a line from a published poem would be used to begin a completely new poem, such as "The prophet digs with iron claws" from the 1938 "Transfiguration," which was used to begin a different verse twenty years (or more) later.

I had no doubt Barnes knew exactly what she was doing when most of these drafts were originally written, but that was anywhere from ten to twenty-five years earlier. She must have had a grand design, but while she was a fine stylist with a distinctive way with words, she obviously lacked the ability or ambition to organize and complete the task she originally envisioned. There were "marvelous lines" everywhere and no lack of dramatic images and themes, but as the years went by the material became more and more disorganized, a situation brought on, in my opinion, not by any lack of ability but rather by her peculiar work habits and decreasing stamina.

Barnes's work habits were very sloppy when I knew her, and the thousands of pages around her apartment indicated it had been the case for years. She could not begin work on a poem, stop, and begin the next day where she had stopped. She began again and again, each page noted again with her name, address, and date. The result was hundreds of versions of the same poems, all retained and mixed up, a draft from 1965 next to one from 1975 and many others mixed in seeming chaos. As years went by the papers piled higher and higher. An added complication was that the pages were all extensively edited. Since those days with Barnes I've seen reproductions of Joyce's handiwork on portions of *Ulysses*, which appeared in *Transition* magazine. The bulk of drafts in Barnes's apartment looked very similar. I don't know whether Joyce used pens and pencils of different colors, but Barnes used red, blue, and green pens, often combining the colors on a single page. Some of the severely edited pages took on a visual life of their own, apart from any literary content.

Another difficulty was the scope of her work; her ideas, while interesting, were not very broad. Ideas and key phrases poured forth over and over again as she created more and more drafts of fairly similar material—but she was not working on ideas that were new to her. A phrase may have been new, or a combination of words fresh, but the themes had been formulated decades earlier. What she needed to edit was now nearly as old as I, and she was simply overwhelmed by the mass of her own creation. She once said to me, "When you're creating it's just you and God—then it's only God. The greatest ecstasy is when you're possessed and don't know why. It isn't like sex, it isn't like anything; nothing is comparable." I'm certain she could still have been creative at 88, but the mass of unorganized paper left her so confused she was only able to contemplate burning her papers or lying in bed screaming at the wall. In early 1979, she didn't really have the option of working on her poems even though she may have tricked herself into believing she did. Almost everything in her life was out of control. She'd rage at the injustice of it all because she didn't want to face the reasons why such things were happening to "poor Miss Barnes." When not raging or endlessly tending to mundane matters, she "played at being a poet," as she put it, editing, revising, or working on verses about animals, totally aware of what she was doing but helpless to do anything about it.

In the early part of 1979 I continued to sort the many drafts while Barnes concerned herself with the possibility of completing her bestiary. I found much that was not only repetitive but also brutal and horrifying. Consider the following lines, each followed by the title, draft, or completed poem from which it is taken:

"The maggots fasten on her breastbone's meat. . . . Death doth make her sing. Death is her King." "Death and the Wood"

"When I came headlong through the bloody door . . . It was my mother naked that I wore. . . ." "Nativity"

". . . a hood of blood we wear, a shirt of skin. . . ." "Lament for Women"

"He lays her carcass on the butt . . . and howls aloud and licks the hand that it reeks of blood. . . ." "Discant (1970)"

"Charge her walking mort, say where she goes . . . she scalds her bush with blood. I buzz the gate. . . ." "Discant"

"I also keep a woman too feeding 'till I get by. . . ." "Alcestis"

Berenice Abbott had once told me her old friend was fond of collecting peculiar religious objects and souvenirs from cemeteries, and had kept them in her Paris apartment. I never noticed any relics in her apartment, but the words and images seem to have remained.

In the 1920s, Barnes had created some wonderfully ribald works, notably *Ryder* and *Ladies Almanack*. The intent of both was semi-serious; each treated the world in general and sex in particular in a rollicking, good-natured way, but none of this remained in any of the work I saw. Consider lines like "When beasts step backward from the acts the scroll of heaven too reacts. . . ."; "What, kiss the famine of an old man's mouth. . . ."; and ". . . buggering with clenched teeth, his monocle gripped in his water rising eye aloft. . . ." Love was present, but it was always hopeless: ". . . all lovers keep some others feeding death. . . ."; ". . . the kiss that festers in the palm. . . ."; and ". . . some still ask what it is to be in love. . . ."

The titles were equally gloomy; "Antique," "A Victim in a State of Decline," "Finis," "Transfiguration," "Lament for Wretches Everyone," and "The Derelict Springs." I read on and on, hoping to find a bit of cheer somewhere, but it was not to be found in her work of the past forty years.

If these were the ideas, the images that were constantly in Barnes's mind, then it was no wonder her outlook on life was so totally dismal. Nor was it surprising that she was unable to sleep at night, why she often spent night after night "crawling up the wall." She often spoke of frightening nights. This dreary imagery and horrible view of life combined with old age, her former problems with alcohol, minor nervous breakdowns, and current drug dependency must have made it difficult to fall asleep and hell once sleep arrived, with various demons, real or imagined, persecuting her at every turn. I don't know how much she was affected by these thoughts in the second half of her life, but I saw their impact in the years I knew her.

Yet, sleep or not, Barnes was making an effort to work at her poetry; we both concluded the bestiary was a task she could complete. She had been working on it since the 1960s. The drafts were at least a foot high, all for twenty-four verses of but four lines each. Two letters, A and Z were not used; A was "Alas" and Z ended the poem; in early drafts it was "zero." The letter X was not an animal but was used anyway.

We organized a complete version, dated 1977. It was titled *Figures in an Alphabet*. It had been dedicated to Mr. Richard Scott Walker, but at some point he had fallen from favor and Barnes had drawn a line through his name. The majority of the animals in this version were those used in the published version of 1982.

Barnes began to make a few changes, first with the title; "figures" was replaced by "creatures"; imago replaced a nonsensical "I and you," the hippo grew to a hippopotamus, the jackass became a jay, and the kinkajou edged out the kangaroo. She made minor alterations to each of the other verses and worried over the use of certain words. One, solfeggio, was of particular concern. I found myself searching for as many sources as possible for its most precise (in Barnes's mind) meaning.

After many false starts she typed a "final" draft, each verse on a separate page, with her name typed and underlined in the upper right hand corner of every one. She did not dedicate it to anyone. Once completed, however, she changed the title back to "figures," made additional minor changes, resurrected the hippo, and considered it completed. She asked me to type a complete draft, following her alterations to the letter. I did not type her name on every page, but this passed her scrutiny. She made a few additional corrections and requested another typed manuscript, which I promptly delivered. It was changed once more. The final version, as requested, used the title *Figures in an Alphabet* and was dedicated to "Emily Coleman, wherever she is."

I used bold type for the final version. She was pleased with it; when we put this version on the shelf it did not contain a single correction. It was ready for publication in her mind, pending the selection of proper illustrations to go with each animal. We then moved on to other, more complicated matters.

The animal verses were published by Dial as *Creatures in an Alphabet* in 1982; there were a number of changes from the "final" 1979 version. The line "wherever she is" was dropped from the dedication; a new four-line verse served as an introduction; three verses from a 1978 draft (the blue jay, ocelot, and peacock) were used; and a new verse about a hummingbird replaced the buffalo. The line which originally followed each verse, "O Mister Physter and Miss Peugh, what is creation coming to" was dropped completely. Barnes died before the book was issued, which was just as well. Though the small volume is charming enough, printed by offset on adequate paper, the illustrations are badly reproduced, in many cases printed out of register (or photographed from the original drawings out of focus). This would have enraged her, and she certainly would have been saddened by the two-inch notice of the book in the *New York Times*, written by Andrew Field. He referred to the book as a "slight work," which indeed it was. Presumably he would have been kinder had she been alive.

Barnes never thought of the poem as anything but a diversion, originally for children. She told me the only lines that were of any consequence were the four she composed for the letter I: imago. In her mind this short verse was dedicated to Dr. Gustave Beck, a highly capable and tolerant physician who treated her on numerous occasions at Lenox Hill Hospital. She was very fond of Dr. Beck, or at least her idealized version of him, and felt these few words were an appropriate indication of her feeling for him. She was also fond of the yak, felt it was a cut above the others and a fitting verse to use in closing.

Her usual working schedule was predictable. I'd normally meet with her in the late afternoon throughout 1979. I'd find her at her desk, working on something, peering through her large magnifying glass, correcting a draft with colored pens or stumpy pencils. She very badly wanted to work, and with the animal poems behind her she began to concentrate on serious poems. She made constant notes and many revisions, but by this time I had organized enough material to begin a folder of potential poems for her consideration. We finally selected forty-seven possible candidates for serious work and set aside another folder for "approved" poems. She quickly approved a few items I had sorted from the piles of papers; these were often left as they were, sometimes slightly revised and re-typed, then noted as "O.K." In some instances she even noted the approval herself, in pencil or with a colored pen. Some poems were noted "U.K. Group" and others "German Group." In the early 1970s she had forwarded two batches of poems to Faber and Faber in the U.K. and Suhrkamp Verlag in Germany, just in case anything might happen to her suddenly. None of these poems were ever published to her knowledge.

The forty-seven poems in the working folder are listed below, noting the first line as it appeared on the working draft, the "Title," if one existed, a date if one existed, and an approval (O.K.). Many of the titles such as "Discant" and "Derelictions" are catchalls; Barnes presumably would have titled each if the process had ever gone that far. Of course, there is the possibility she felt she could complete the entire project.

1. All children at some time go hand in hand. "The Bo Tree/ Dereliction." Noted as O.K. in 1979.
2. And should I mourn, and should I. "Epiphany," 10 February 1974.
3. As whales by dolphins slashed bring on a school. "Lament for Wretches Everyone."

4. At eight in the morning when the ladies came. "Magnificent Canticle."
5. And others say: "What is it to be possessed."
6. Because a lady made me and woe for that I fell into that sullen lake.
7. Call her walking mort, say where she goes. "Call Her Walking Mort," first part of "Dereliction," then "Discant" (O.K.).
8. Cold comfort she made of it I said.
9. Death and the maid have got him in their stall. "The Great Man."
10. Does the inch worm on the atlas mourn? "Dereliction" (O.K.).
11. For rustibus there should be shaws. "Dereliction."
12. Had I the foresight of the mole. "Dereliction" (Augusta said).
13. He said to the Don, "My Lord your dangling man's not crucified he's gored." "Discant" (O.K.).
14. His mother said who long since in her mother is been hid. "Discant."
15. If electric fields our plots destroy. "Who Died That Day at Danamora/Who Was It Died That Day at Alcatraz"/ "Laughing Lamentations."
16. In this season of the lost salvation.
17. Look not upon her jealousy.
18. Lord, what is man that he was once you brag. "Alas How Are the Rosaries Broken Down"/"Laughing Lamentations."
19. Man cannot purge his body of its theme. "Rites of Spring," 13 July 1979.
20. On my spade I'll bring her home. "Dereliction" (part of this poem is also in "Pharaoh").
21. Over in the meadow, in the sand, in the sun.

22. See how the sledded tongue reams out her mouth. "Derelictions."
23. Sing now a land for rank aged men.
24. So they went up and down mainly crying. "Obsiequies," 25 March 1974.
25. Some still ask "what's it to be in love." "The Phantom and the Predator," 13 July 1973/5 February 1978 (O.K.).
26. Tell where is the kissing crust. "Dereliction"/"Virgin Spring."
27. The blood of the Lamb and oriflame. "Galerie Religieuse." (The version printed in 1962) (O.K.).
28. The prophet digs with iron claws.
29. There is no gender in the fossil's eye. "Discant" or "Of Dereliction, Parthenogenesis and Phantom Spring."
30. There is no swarming in him now.
31. There should be a garden for old men to twitter in. "Discant."
32. There should be gaboons for men to roll against audacity.
33. Therefore daughter of the glen. "Dereliction."
34. Therefore: Look not upon her horizontally. "Discant," September 1970.
35. Therefore sisters now begin. "Therefore Sisters," 13 August 1974 (O.K.).
36. There's that truth that only victims savour. "A Victim Is a State of Decline," 1 February 1974.
37. Think on Ramses no wake wag these. "Pharaoh" (O.K.).
38. When at my hour I think to hop the twig. "Dereliction (Now the Obsequies Begin)."
39. When beasts step backward from the acts. "Dereliction."
40. When I came headlong through the bloody door. "Nativity/ Viaticum," 25 August 1974.
41. When I first saw my fable it was grazing.
42. When the kissing flesh is gone. "Dereliction" (O.K.).

43. When riderless a horse is seen. "Descent/The Coupling" (O.K.).
44. When unhors'd a ghost is seen. "Discant."
45. While I unwind duration from the tongie-tied tree. "Quarry."
46. With what fastidious alarm he fells his fly. "Dereliction."
47. Who does not love the chorister? "Who is Sylvia" (Submitted to *The New Yorker* and rejected by them in July 1971.).

The small folder reserved for final, approved drafts did not grow very quickly, and as the days passed it became clear it probably wouldn't in the near future. It was not from lack of trying; Barnes worked at it and I encouraged her as much as possible, but pain, lack of stamina, and assorted diversions took their toll. She was right when she told me, "I can't write anymore. The spark is gone. Do you think it goes on forever? Do you think you can write *Nightwood* in a minute?" On 13 July she typed a draft of *Rite of Spring*, the major poem she had been developing and condensing for thirty years. To my knowledge she never typed another complete version of it. I found it on her desk after I had checked her into Lenox Hill Hospital. Asked why she left it on her desk, she replied it was "just in case" anything went wrong. A great deal did go wrong during that stay, but it was not at the hospital.

Barnes's apartment was very old, poorly wired, and badly plumbed. The building was less than twenty feet wide, the stairs listed badly, the rooms were very small. There was a two-room apartment on the first floor, two on the second (Barnes had the front), and at least one on the third floor. A gentleman on that floor, unknown to me but referred to by Barnes as "the leather-clad pansy," decided to install some new bathroom fixtures. Whatever he did went wrong. She was recovering from a urinary infection at Lenox Hill Hospital when something on the third floor either burst or overflowed, above Barnes's small back room. As the water worked its way through the plaster it finally reached the electrical wiring, which shorted and began to smoke. The smoke was noted by the people on the first floor and they dutifully called the fire brigade. They also called me, knowing Barnes was in the hospital. When I arrived the firemen had already made their way into Barnes's apartment, breaking through the protective grate covering her window. Everything in the back room was soaked, the ceiling was collapsing in many places, there was no electricity, and the ceiling in the main room was beginning to crumble. I had removed almost everything in the back room as soon as Barnes checked into Lenox Hill and taken it, carefully boxed and marked, to my studio. The small one-time storage area had been made ready, complete with bed and chair, for the nurse we both felt was necessary when she returned from the hospital.

Extensive renovations became the order of the day—fixing the electricity, plastering, painting, drying out the new bed, and general cleaning. Jussi was a wonder, he did a spectacular job, and everything was ready for Barnes when she finally returned; in fact it was better than when she left. The walls were a fresh blue, thirty years of dust were gone from the books on the top shelves. Yet, as I looked about the room in its original state of chaos I could only imagine what would have happened had Barnes been present with the water, smoke, and collapsing ceilings. How would she have reacted as the firemen came through the window? The last time anyone had done this, a burglar, she had cracked him over the head with a stick.

My other concern was what if the place had burned? When I surveyed the damage I spotted the two folders of approved and working poems. If the building was going to burn down I'd be happier if there was a copy of these pages somewhere else. I took the last version of *Rite of Spring*, put it into a folder, and made my way to a good copy machine. I returned the originals the following day and placed the copies in a file at my studio. This action was ultimately irrelevant but it made me feel much better at the time. When Barnes returned from the hospital and I told her what I had done, she was typically unconcerned that I had the copies in my file. She was out of commission for some while as she recovered from the rigors of Lenox Hill.

Barnes was in no mood to work on her poetry when she returned from the hospital. The minor urinary tract infection had been easy to treat, but she was very weak and her apartment was decidedly "new." Instead of writing she talked about it, which was always easier, and from this time forward she was at her desk less and less. It wasn't just the distractions; she was tired and it was so much easier to do anything other than write. She once said, "There have only been two things in my life that made me truly happy and both were aborted, but I could always be happy whenever I could strike a line I liked." She had little opportunity in late 1979 to strike likeable lines but she was often very happy talking about those she had written years earlier.

Barnes was not fond of her first published works: the newspaper articles, short plays, stories, and assorted poems. Newspaper work was merely a job, words written for hire, to support herself and, to a degree, some of her family. She considered the work trivial and it concerned her when someone reprinted an article or poem she had written sixty or more years earlier. The plays from the same period also troubled her; she felt them immature and derivative. There were a few plays, some known, others unpublished in her files, short, one-act plays, but there was one fragment of longer effort.

She was convinced they should be burned but never had the heart to do it. She was probably correct; I read two of these early works, found them dull, and told her so. She knew of their inadequacies but, published or not, a number of them were performed at the time they were written.

She was also aware of their content. In 1980, she received an inquiry from a gentleman asking about some details of one that had been performed in 1919. As I read the letter to Barnes she evidenced her usual mock outrage. How could this person assume she remembered such trivial matters about a play that was no more than inconsequential nonsense? She settled down after a moment and proceeded to tell me all about it, including minor production details and the color of costumes. She didn't feel it necessary to pass it on to the man who inquired, but I did so and merely kept it a secret.

The poems were another matter; many of them had been published, and she had saved copies of magazines and pages from newspapers and periodicals in which they had appeared. I gathered many of these scattered pages, just in case she wanted to include any of her early work in the projected volume of poetry, which was growing slimmer by the day. She had retained copies of twenty-one early poems, plus those that appeared in her first "book," the short illustrated pamphlet-sized publication, *The Book of Repulsive Women*.

The plan to issue a small volume of poems never developed sufficiently to even consider inclusion of any of the early work, but my suspicion is that Barnes would have rejected almost all of it. She hated *The Book of Repulsive Women*, saying, "My first book of poems is a disgusting little item. At one time in the 1920s I collected as many copies as I could find and burned them in my mother's backyard." I told her I had once seen one advertised for

$750, and she was outraged. I don't know whether her reaction was because of the price, because someone had had a copy for sale, or because she had contributed to the rarity of the booklet by burning so many copies. It is clear, however, that she disliked most of her early poetry. Only one of her pre-1920 efforts, "Antique" (1918), was included in her anthology-like 1923 issue, *A Book*; it was retained when this book was reissued in 1929 as *A Night Among the Horses*.

Barnes's last published early poem was issued in 1923, but it is clear that she continued to write in this form, even though her next publication was in 1936. She was silent once more until 1958, but drafts of poems with Paris, London, and New York addresses were scattered throughout her papers. It is unclear whether she ever attempted to do anything with these earlier drafts, but it is more than likely she didn't attempt to publish any of them. She rarely discussed these old poems and often said, "I can't remember one verse I have ever written." I knew this wasn't the case for newer work, but it was undoubtedly true for sixty-five year old relics.

Barnes regarded her early stories with equal disdain. They were produced to earn a living and not to be seriously considered by anyone, including herself. They were a matter of concern only when someone wished to reprint them, as did the Phoenix Book Shop with *Greenwich Village As It Is*, and in 1979 when Sun and Moon announced plans to publish a collection of her early stories under the title of *A Night in the Woods*.

I had discovered the planned publication by the small press from a flyer at a book fair. I knew she would be annoyed if I told her about it, that it would result in more wasted time, but I also felt it was sufficiently important to advise her of it. She was considerably more distressed than I had anticipated. The end result was an extended period of despair and rage. Someone was taking her work to be sure, but the primary problem was that they were, in her mind, trespassing on *Nightwood*. Her point was well taken; the short story, "A Night in the Woods" was published in a 1917 edition of the *New York Morning Telegram Sunday Magazine*, one story among many in the book planned by Sun and Moon. I sympathized with Barnes but suspected little could be done to stop publication. Early on in the crisis a friend put me in touch with the former Attorney General Ramsey Clark; a short conversation produced a fine plan: advise the publishers that we knew it was impossible to stop publication, but the use of the proposed title could be judged both misleading and injurious to Barnes's reputation. If the book was published with the title as planned, Barnes would take whatever legal actions might be necessary to protect her interests.

There was no possibility that she would ever appear in court; not only was she disinclined to do so, but she was not physically able to consider it. The publishers were most decent about it, and in retrospect perhaps I may have acted too harshly. They changed their plans, held the book until after Barnes's death, and issued it under the title *Smoke*. Barnes, however, was able to see the action as a victory on her part and was pleased to have been able to halt what to her was an illegal edition of her work.

Barnes's three major works of the 1920s were of little concern to her at the end of her life. The stories she felt were worthwhile, all written and published in the 1920s, had been revised and issued in final form as *Spillway* by Faber and Faber of England in 1962. All but one also appeared in *Selected Works*, issued the same year in the United States. She rarely discussed any of them, other than to say "Aller et Retour" was the finest.

Ladies Almanack (Barnes normally referred to it in correspondence and conversation as "The" *Ladies Almanack*) and *Ryder* were both published in 1928; it is unclear which was issued first but both were similar in style. Barnes never referred to the reason why she chose to adopt the peculiar style found in these two works but made it clear to me she regarded *Ladies Almanack* as frivolous and *Ryder* only slightly better. She often remarked, "It will be my fate to be remembered for the *Ladies Almanack*."

The book was written as a diversion, for both Barnes and Thelma Wood, who was hospitalized at the time. It poked fun at Natalie Barney and some of her coterie, but was never intended as a serious work. She often expressed amazement that anyone regarded it as anything but a trifle. This may have been a pose on Barnes's part; when it was reissued by Harper and Row in 1972 she wrote an appropriately convoluted foreword and at some point considered revising portions of it. I saw at least one new manuscript page among her papers with the heading "new page for *Ladies Almanack*."

Most of Barnes's comments about the book referred to physical production, selling it in Paris cafes, hand-coloring some copies (a task she did herself, with the assistance of Tylia Perlmutter), her fight with the "publisher" Edward Titus (whose name she crossed out when she signed copies of the original edition), and the fact that many copies were hidden away in the far reaches of Morocco. She never revealed why the copies were in North Africa or how they got there, but she was astounded when I purchased copy number one thousand in a Washington, D.C. bookshop. The pages were uncut; it was still in its glassine container. She wondered if someone had possibly found the stash of books in Morocco and felt it was appropriate for me to have the "last," which had made its way back to her after so many years. A short while later she gave me one of the colored copies, which was of less interest to her than the "last" one.

Barnes took pride in *Ryder*'s having made its way to the best-seller lists in 1928, if only for a moment. The book in that year was considered slightly scandalous; she was certain the ribald excesses made it sell and she was well aware of the kind of book she was writing before she signed a contract with her publisher.

The manuscript for *Ryder* was complete prior to August 1927, the date of her contract with Liveright, which specified "the publisher agrees to make all cuts necessary to *Ryder* to enable it to appear in America and indicate every excision by the insertion of asterisks." Both Barnes and Liveright knew precisely what they were doing with *Ryder*, but it is interesting to note that Liveright did not anticipate such quick initial sales. It is even more interesting that Barnes was willing to let her publisher make cuts at will in her manuscript.

Paris,
1926

*E*ven though she was later convinced it sold well because of its ribald content, it is unlikely that she wrote it with sales in mind. The contract only called for a five hundred dollar advance and a planned first edition of three thousand copies. This edition sold out quickly; it made the best seller lists, but then there was no stock available. Liveright rushed a second edition into print the next month, but by then demand had diminished and there was little call for the second printing. The result was a common first edition and a scarce second. Barnes didn't even own a copy of the second, which featured a new dust jacket and eliminated the foreword dealing with censorship, which she had written in August 1927. This foreword was eliminated in the 1979 reissue as well.

Nightwood, the next and last novel, was published eight years later and Barnes had a great deal to say about it. In fact, the book was on her mind all the time and she considered it the cornerstone of her literary career. It was unusual for a day to pass when *Nightwood* didn't figure in our conversations; in her mind the book had a life of its own and was far more important than its creator.

She told me the title came from William Blake's "Tyger, tyger, burning bright in the forests of the night . . . ," and that Thelma Wood had nothing to do with its selection. She rarely spoke of exactly when it was written or the circumstances that compelled her to create it. To be sure, she often spoke of Dan Mahoney, Thelma Wood, Henrietta Metcalf, and all the other "real" people characterized in *Nightwood*, but didn't deal with specific incidents, other than a few that she wished to have me remember. The final scene was crucial and it annoyed her that many people thought the girl and the dog were sexually engaged. She told me repeatedly the girl was drunk, the dog confused, and that she had witnessed the scene herself. It involved her friend "Fitzie" (M. E. Fitzgerald) and her dog Buff. The section with Dr. O'Connor in bed, dressed as a woman, was not exactly as it happened but it was not too far from the truth. She also made it abundantly clear she didn't transcribe any of Dan Mahoney's dialogues, but did use his ideas rather freely.

There was more than one version of the book; Barnes's contract with Liveright in 1927 gave them exclusive right to her next two books after *Ryder*. *A Night Among the Horses* was published by Liveright, partially satisfying the contract, but the company never published a second, which, in terms of chronology, should have been *Nightwood*. Barnes told me they had rejected an early version of her novel in 1931 and showed me the correspondence to prove it. The first version was entitled *Bow Down*, and it was this action that gave Barnes a clear conscience to deal with Faber and Faber in 1936. Liveright complained when the book was published in England and made a feeble effort to prevent publication in the United States in 1937, but with no success.

Barnes lived for *Nightwood*; it had made her literary reputation, and one of a more personal nature as well. She was pleased by the literary praise but annoyed with the personal inferences drawn by others, particularly "weeping lesbians" who called to her from the courtyard or even in her hallway. An attack on the literary merits of the book, or even a lukewarm response to it, was viewed by Barnes as a personal affront and ample cause to do battle with critics and sever ties with long-time associates. Yet, with all her passion and haughty attitude, she was ultimately insecure about it. Just as she would often wonder aloud how she ever had the talent to write, she would also become filled with self doubt if anyone suggested it might be flawed. When *Selected Works* was reissued in 1982, a handful of reviews were forthcoming and a few were not complimentary. I was concerned about her seeing poor reviews and tried to screen them. I knew she might see a review if it was written in the (London) *Times Literary Supplement*, but it was easy to stop the rest. The problem was that, for whatever reason, certain people sent her copies of poor reviews and on any number of occasions such notice in an inconsequential journal by a third-rate academic would send her into a depression that might last for weeks. After one particularly dreary, unsolicited review arrived in the mail, one that complained about her punctuation, she looked at me with a mixture of horror and frustration, and said, "Nobody understands my book. Was the punctuation wrong? I told Tom to edit it, that I didn't know how to do it. He knew I couldn't spell or punctuate. Now, is my masterpiece ruined?" She was sufficiently insecure to allow a silly review to upset her and no matter what I might say, she'd worry, lose sleep, and be agitated. She knew the people writing about her were, for the most part, minor academics or failed writers or both: people to be held in low esteem. But she worried all the same.

I once told her most of her problems with critics might be traced to her advanced age; she had lived too long, outlived almost all her contemporaries, and most people writing the reviews that annoyed her were not even alive when *Nightwood* was first published. Since she was a somewhat mysterious cult figure, most contemporary critics spent as much time reviewing her life as her books. It was much easier to review her life, glamorous and tinged with mystery, than to do a serious appraisal of a complex book or play. Even the most knowledgeable critics reviewed Barnes the person. When the *New York Times Book Review* asked Andre Field, who had just written the biography *Djuna*, to review both *Smoke* and *Creatures in an Alphabet*, at least 90 percent of his review was about Barnes; commentary on the two books was minimal.

One harmless though negative review of *Selected Works* (and *Nightwood* in particular) prompted her to exclaim, "This is a shitty review. Some of (*Nightwood*) may be a little overblown and even a bit pretentious, but most of it is simply marvelous. It is almost like Shakespeare. But no one wants to read things that are complicated anymore. They want silly, easy things. Everyone is giving it to me in the neck. At this stage of my life I don't need this; I might as well just commit suicide." I was trying to prevent this kind of reaction by shielding her from unfavorable reviews that served no useful purpose.

Barnes's usual response to any criticism of her masterpiece was a mixture of rage and despair, which usually modified to a wish to be left alone; "Why don't they just leave me alone?" she'd ask me over and over. It was sad to see her in this condition; we both knew she had created the situation herself, first with the book and then the decision to live the last half of her life in isolation. But this didn't make it any less depressing to see this proud and strong-willed woman reduced to such a state by an academic review.

Barnes was normally tough, argumentative, and unwavering. Yet, when someone she didn't know, someone with limited credentials at best, attacked her work, she would become enraged and eventually wilted into despair. This kind of reaction showed a weakness I had not expected; she was probably far more sensitive than anyone believed. She could mask her feeling with statements like "You have to know a great deal to be a critic; there have, therefore, rarely been any good ones so I don't really pay attention to any." Yet I never saw anything take such a toll on her resources. Possibly the fear of unfavorable criticism and resulting depression may have been the reason she wrote so little after *Nightwood* and remained withdrawn. What little she did publish was written in such an obscure and complicated way as to be beyond the grasp of any critic. In the fall of 1980 when we were considering questions for a proposed *Paris Review* interview (Appendix III), I suggested this might be an excellent topic to consider and she agreed.

It was much more interesting to watch her defend her work, which she did with relish. There were many opportunities to watch her in action. One incident involved a young poet named Peter Klappert, who had written a series of apocryphal poetic monologues and published them with the title *Non Sequitur O'Connor*. The O'Connor in the title was none other than Matthew O'Connor of *Ryder* and *Nightwood*. Barnes was incensed. He had "stolen" her character and, even worse, planned to continue using him in a longer series of monologues entitled *The Idiot Princess of the Last Dynasty*. She raged. Should she take him to court? Who was the "idiot princess?" What a horrid title for a poem! She would look at me and repeat the story about "some fool" who had once gone to Paris after *Nightwood* was published and attempted to write down Dan Mahoney's ramblings, assuming a great book could be written quickly. Here was someone who had not even gone that far. He was inventing Mahoney's ramblings!

It didn't matter to Barnes that Klappert held *Nightwood* and its author in high esteem and in his own way was offering homage with his poem. She could not see beyond the "theft" of her character and the defiling of her masterpiece. It became my duty to write stern letters on her behalf. I read a complimentary foreword that was to be included; the book was to be dedicated to Barnes. The dedication was heartfelt; the commentary on *Nightwood* was passionate. Barnes was having none of it and the end result was the removal of the dedication, the praise of *Nightwood*, and holding publication of the book until after her death. It was finally published in 1984.

I once told Barnes that Dan Mahoney was not her creation, that she had even told me Robert McAlmon used him first; Mahoney was not like Mickey Mouse, a character with a copyright. Nothing made any difference, but the real tragedy of a circumstance such as this was it was so unsettling that it took two months out of her life, when she had few remaining. A situation like this made any kind of serious work impossible, an excuse not to work, not to write, and even though she began to feel somewhat better in the fall and winter of 1979, it became increasingly difficult for me to keep her on track.

The Antiphon was Barnes's last major published work. It was autobiographical, as were all her extended works, and was the subject of intense concern during the years I knew her, causing many more problems than unfavorable reviews of *Nightwood*. The novel, after all, was only subject to reviews and occasional requests for motion picture or dramatic rights, which, of course, were always refused. *The Antiphon* was being considered for production in Switzerland, and this was a matter of some gravity. The difficulties surrounding the planned production were, as usual, her fault.

There were two versions of the play. The first was published in 1958 by the British firm of Faber and Faber, with a simultaneous edition in the United States using sheets printed in England. The play was also included in *Selected Works* in 1962, but in the four years since the original issue Barnes had made considerable revisions and preferred the new version to the old. This always led to confusion, for she was never certain which version anyone had read or was considering.

The second, more serious difficulty was the complexity of the play, its unsuitability for the stage. Barnes referred to her creation as a "closet-drama" and told me any number of times she never intended it to be performed. The result was limited interest in production.

There was one production, the reading at Harvard, prior to publication in 1956. The audience was limited as was the rehearsal time allowed to the student actors. The selected audience of Barnes, T. S. Eliot, and Edwin Muir became very quiet as the production progressed, and the consensus was that the reading was a failure, but a few years later an enthusiastic Edwin Muir told United Nations Secretary General Dag Hammarskjold about Barnes, *Nightwood*, and the play. Hammarskjold was sufficiently impressed with all three to become a good friend of Barnes, to translate the play into Swedish (the first version), and to assist in arranging a production in Stockholm. This was probably the crowning event of Barnes's later years; the play was well-received, she treasured the production stills, and a specially bound, inscribed translation of the play was on the bookshelf next to her bed. The book meant a great deal to her and was the only one in her apartment she wanted included with her papers at the McKeldin Library.

There was little other interest, even though Suhrkamp Verlag, Barnes's West German publishers, said they wanted to translate and publish it in 1961. I know few of the particulars but from Barnes's comments and the limited correspondence in her files, it was clear a translation was undertaken and completed by the late 1960s. The work was done by two women who lived in Rome, Inge von Weidenbaum and Christine Koschel, who, because they posted their letters from the Vatican were always referred to by Barnes as "the girls from the Vatican." Whether the translation was ever published is unclear. I never saw a copy among Barnes's books and don't recall royalty statements, but when I began assisting her, the translation had been in existence for some time.

In all the years I knew her, Barnes was in a quandary over a proposed German-language production of the play. It was a problem when I met her and remained so when I left. One difficulty was the translation itself that the director, Swiss-based Werner Duggelin, disliked. He wanted to translate the play himself but Barnes, despite her fondness for him, felt some loyalty to the "girls in the Vatican." She couldn't read the translation but suspected it was "mushy" because the letters from her translators and the limited personal contact she'd had with one of them indicated they were much too fond of her personally. Barnes and I got along because I didn't worship her words; she was suspicious of anyone, particularly any female, who seemed to her overly enthusiastic.

The attempted production was a little drama itself, unfortunately tending toward soap opera: a constant flow of letters, pleading from the Vatican, urgent requests from Duggelin, confusion on the part of Suhrkamp, and Barnes's procrastination. Speaking no German, she was helpless to evaluate any translation, a situation complicated by Barnes's inability to remember which version had been translated; she hoped it was the second but could not be certain. We both suspected the Suhrkamp version was taken from the first, given the time frame of their initial interest. Duggelin had said this version was pretentious. Those words became etched in stone; Barnes wondered whether the second version was just as pretentious. It was all very confusing to me, and Barnes finally became so frustrated that she advised Duggelin to do anything he wished, but to get on with the production and consult whenever possible with her old friend and translator of *Nightwood*, Wolfgang Hildesheimer.

There were more delays, but in 1980 I arranged for a young lady from Germany to visit Barnes, and one result of their meeting was surprising. She was personally acquainted with many actors in Germany, including some who she knew were being considered for Duggelin's production. She promised Barnes she'd supply her with photographs of some of the actors. When they arrived Barnes was horrified; everyone was unattractive and ill-suited for her play, but she remained silent at this point. Months passed, nothing happened; the correspondence was dwindling. I doubt that there ever was a production; nothing had happened when Barnes and I parted company in mid-1981.

Everything regarding *The Antiphon* had been a waste, my work for a few years and Barnes's for some while longer. She worried for days about Duggelin's production, his offending the "girls in the Vatican," and other trivialities. All these things were merely added diversions, which unfortunately prevented her from working.

When not writing or talking about what she had written in the past, Barnes and I were concerned about keeping in print everything she had written and arranging new publications in overseas markets. The United States was under control with the publication of *Ryder* in 1979 and *Selected Works* in 1980. She was pleased with both books, particularly the handsome new edition of *Selected Works*; it was larger than the first version, and the dust jacket was far superior. She was unconcerned that *Ladies Almanack* was out of print; for her so much the better. If it was out of sight it would ease her fears of being remembered for a trivial book.

The situation in Europe was in shambles. Her overseas affairs had long been handled by Faber and Faber, but little had been done in recent years. When she instructed me to begin arranging for overseas editions she gave me a slim folder of correspondence to and from Peter du Sautoy, then (1969–71) Vice-Chairman of Faber and Faber. A quick reading of the letters told all. On 3 March 1969, Barnes wrote to her friend and publisher du Sautoy:

'When I do count the clock that tells the time, and see the brave day sunk' in this March date of exactly the third day, in answer to yours of September 26th, I presume it is folly to be wise—in short, I could wish a great number of my writings had managed to avoid being written—but T.S.E. himself advised, when Farrar, Straus was preparing to bring out my *Selected Works*, that I give them all. He said they'd be found out at a later date anyway, providing I was remembered, I reminded him that *The Sacred Wood* was one he was glad to have out of print. He replied: 'THAT was a work of critical nature.' I don't know that there is such a great difference between the objections, one perhaps would disoblige other people, the other little or no credit to myself. However some of my things have been pirated, *The Ladies Almanack* (which you did get back from Neske, tho not *Ryder*) could very easily be, as, like a fool, I did not have it copyrighted in France.

There is one catch about *Ryder*. The Liveright publishing corporation who took over Horace Liveright's publishing house (taken over from Boni and Liveright I don't recall the date) when it went bankrupt, now has really no right to keep *Ryder* and *A Book* (Giroux said so). Giroux tried to break his back when he did publish my *Selected Works*, but that case got nowhere as later, I balked at going into court against New Directions. You have all that dreadful hashed up mess, in the file if you have kept my correspondence. Giroux and Straus said we could take *Nightwood* away from New Directions, if you recall. I said I would not deny the good faith permission given them, etc, etc. As for Pell I don't know what they did with him. You must have all those too among the Barnes papers!

In general the whole thing horrifies me with the thought of seeing all that paper and print again! Does Suhrkamp want *A Book*, its reissue *A Night Among the Horses*? (I don't think we should let him have the *A Book* thing, with drawings, which were not taken into the *Night Among the Horses*). And what of the privately printed *Ladies Almanack*? That would have to have pictures. *Ryder*? Also illustrated. What would he do with these? and *Nightwood*, both with Neske and Fischer???

And my new work, a small clutch of poetry? When will that get done, if I get into a snarl with publishers?

Of course its delightful to think anyone cares about publishing anything. By the By, Wolfgang Hildesheimer has been a charming creature, wrote me he would look over the German translation now being made of *The Antiphon*, and would speak to the young ladies when in Rome in this month, or in April. And in general he would do his best to get my work put about. I thank him, and anyone who has affection for my written word! Didn't you tell me Mr. Suhrkamp wanted *Spillway*?

So let me hear what you think. Please. Has the annual subscription been paid the Society of Authors and why do I belong? I have forgotten.

Two pages written in 1969 told the entire story. Reading them ten years later I realized almost nothing had happened with the books, the "small clutch of poetry," or scarcely anything else. A glance at the letters that followed revealed du Sautoy trying to be as accommodating as possible in arranging for European publications but finally in despair asking in 1971, "If you won't believe me whom will you believe?"

Barnes responded with a long letter explaining how she had gone back to old contracts and correspondence in storage and proved she was correct in all her assertions. The result was that nothing happened; when I stumbled into Barnes's life, *nothing* had become a constant in her life. Faber and Faber were still her publishers, but they were doing little with a sense of urgency or much enthusiasm. I wasn't surprised. Barnes's last line in the last letter in the file was: "I am exhausted with all these matters," and I wasn't surprised by that either. It was easy to become exhausted; the third or fourth reading of a long contract alone would do it every time. Yet, for all these difficulties it eventually became easy for me to arrange for overseas publication; by 1981, contracts were signed for the principal European markets for almost all Barnes's major works and some of her minor ones. Faber and Faber continued in England, France was divided between Editions du Seuil and Ernst Flammarion, Suhrkamp continued taking her books in Germany, Italy was divided between Bompiani and Adelphi, and new publishers were found in Spain, Finland, Sweden, Denmark, and the Netherlands. It was particularly gratifying to license the *Ladies Almanack*; anyone could have just appropriated it.

Barnes had tried desperately to place her work in the 1960s, with almost no success. She felt she should be well-paid for her work, as she certainly should have been, but this was not what caused the difficulty. It was one thing to drive a hard bargain but quite another to drive a potential publisher up the wall with delays, concerns about forty-year-old contracts, miscellaneous details, and rewriting contracts to reflect a 2 percent motion picture royalty rate instead of merely one. Barnes was so frustrated by the inactivity and seeming hopelessness of the situation that her attitude had become "Who cares, what does it matter if they survive?" It was not difficult to take it easy with the publishers; they were generally eager for the books if it wasn't too much of a problem, and I tried to make certain it remained easy. The contracts arrived, were signed within a week, and when eventually an advance check would arrive, Barnes would be pleased. As we followed the progress on the large chart it was easy to see who had which book, the status of the contract, advance payment, or publication date. I assumed more and more responsibility for overseeing this activity; I wanted to see every blank filled in on the chart in Barnes's lifetime and as she was less and less able to concentrate on contracts, I merely did them on my own. Of course, this ultimately proved to be a serious error on my part. I suspected it would eventually cause difficulties, but the truth is there was no other way to handle the situation with reasonable efficiency.

I wanted Barnes to write, wanted the relationship to produce something more than conversation, but it was not to be; reality turned out to be thousands of spoken words, not written. The limited time Barnes devoted to her work produced little finished poetry. My grand plan for a small book was ultimately a failure.

Yet, if my original plan had been to organize Barnes's life sufficiently to allow her the leisure and freedom from worry and from the immediate threat of illness to write, another important part of the plan was to bring her into contact with a few, carefully selected new people and fresh ideas: to open her long-closed front door to the outside world. Consequently, I brought a few people by and was always forgetting books, magazines, and cassettes, hoping someone or something might make a difference. The fresh ideas and printed material worked well; I was less successful with the people.

Barnes was pessimistic in her writing, and most of her general beliefs were gloomy. She felt most people were vile, insufferable charlatans, or stupid. Some manifested only a few of these characteristics; she thought most had all of them. It was easy for her to find fault with almost everyone, which made it difficult to find appropriate visitors. The people I took by to introduce to her were those I thought she'd find interesting, young ladies who might be able to help her in my absence and the occasional young female writer who contacted me, usually pleading for an opportunity to meet the legendary Barnes. The young ladies were carefully screened, thoroughly briefed on the topics to avoid in their conversation and how to act when and if the audience was granted.

Barnes really didn't want to see anyone, it was much easier to maintain her mysterious aura if she avoided everyone. Her natural animosity towards successful women complicated matters. I was never certain whether she felt insecure with other women in the arts besides writers or just felt the only creative or interpretive process worth considering was literature. The fact is that she regarded most of the successful women I introduced to her as threatening or uninteresting or both and never wanted to see them again. I could have brought a great doctor, a noted painter, or a fine actress. If the person was female she'd find a way to denigrate her accomplishments. This pertained to female friends as well. I can't recall her ever being complimentary about many females who were not writers, and she could be harsh with the writers too. Of all the women I took to visit her, only one, Maggie Condon, was ever asked to return; in that instance the two became close friends.

It was probably easier for Barnes to interact with men, but because I found so few to introduce her to it was difficult to reach any general conclusion on this point. She was extremely eager to meet the Swedish-born, Swiss-based film director, Erwin Leiser. I told her he had not only seen the production of *The Antiphon* in Stockholm, but had reviewed it favorably for a Swedish newspaper. He was the only person she ever encountered who had not only seen the play but understood it. She looked forward to his visit, and their meeting was long and friendly. Leiser admired her and she was obviously touched; she happily signed his copy of *Nightwood*, and had the opportunity arisen she would have been pleased to see him again. Other men, however, did not fare so well. She was particularly rude to a noted actor I took along on a visit. She felt he was presumptuous because he sat on the end of her bed for part of the visit. There was no other place for him to sit; one chair was at the upholsterers, but that was irrelevant. She expected him to stand.

*This photo may have been
taken by Thelma Wood,
France, 1925*

A number of young women were willing to lend a hand;
they were not budding writers nor people who wished to discuss
the lesbian overtones of *Nightwood*; they were simply nice people,
eager to be kind. Perhaps they were interested in a close look at one
of the few living legends left in Greenwich Village, but any such
ulterior motives stopped there.

When business took me out of town it was necessary to have someone on call at all times to aid Barnes if a crisis arose. There was never a genuine crisis in my absence, but once an imagined one led to an almost ridiculous situation. I was away for a day when she accidentally dropped one of her dental plates. It cracked and she was certain she'd starve to death if it was not repaired immediately. She looked at the paper I'd left her, dialed the crisis number for that day, and reached Karen Kraft, a young rock singer, who responded promptly, took time out from her schedule to deliver the badly broken plate to a dentist, waited for a hasty repair, and returned with it to the agitated Barnes. Barnes was not well acquainted with Karen but thought little of her vocal abilities. She was, however, friendly when Karen returned and gave her a check for the repair. Later in the day Karen telephoned to make certain the plate was holding up. Barnes replied it was as good as could be expected, but she had chest pains and it was becoming difficult to breathe. She thought she might not last the night and wasn't it just her luck the last person she might ever speak with was a "dreadful rock and roll singer." My crisis list was diminished by one.

Lesbian writers were another matter. Few gained access to her, yet Barnes enjoyed the few who managed. They praised her wildly, but had been briefed to mention nothing with even vague sexual overtones. I never told these women what to say, only what subjects to avoid. Barnes was loathe to discuss sexual matters with strangers and was uninterested in meeting anyone who wanted to consider lesbian nuances in her work. She had made it clear to me that she would never have written *Nightwood* if she'd known the reputation it would bring her, and she also made it clear she had no interest in changing anyone's life. "I don't want to make a lot of little lesbians," she'd often say. I made certain all the young female writers were aware of her feelings; they played by the rules and usually managed to have a good visit with their heroine. That she professed opinions surprising to them was of little importance; some even managed to correspond with her for a short while.

All these people were just temporary diversions for Barnes; I soon realized I had become the primary one, but it was not difficult to entertain or be entertained by her. She found almost any written word interesting on some level, so anything I might have in my bag would fascinate her for a minute and stimulate conversation. Current events or any kind of wild theory had the same effect. I knew this distracted from her work, but I also knew a lively conversation would take her mind off her troubles. Our conversations usually took place toward the end of the day when I was aware that she had no intention of doing anything else at her desk.

Intolerant though she was of many ideas and theories, she nonetheless enjoyed discussing them. It was amazing to witness how quickly she could grasp matters outside her normal interests: politics, science, social problems. She had an opinion on a variety of subjects, often based on limited knowledge, but naturally an interesting viewpoint. She was particularly acute in understanding artistic matters.

One day I had a book with me that dealt with the noted Colombian painter, Fernando Botero. She was fascinated with his work; she thought it was spectacular and wanted to see every book I had that dealt with him. I told her I had many and also knew him slightly, having photographed him. She had to see the photographs, but when I brought them by she was certain he was far too handsome to have painted the pictures in the books. She forgot what he looked like and concentrated on his work; he was truly marvelous. High praise indeed from the stern Miss Barnes.

She also expressed interest in a book of photographs by Walker

Evans that I left with her. As I departed she was examining each photograph very carefully with her magnifying glass, looking at the details. The next day we talked about Evans. She liked his photograph of Hart Crane but not the one of Berenice Abbott. A photograph of a graveyard fascinated her; in her mind it was the best in the book, but she was puzzled by the placement of Evans's camera. She said he should have waited until the sun moved and shifted the shadows. It was a perceptive comment from someone who held photography in such contempt. The broken 1915-vintage Kodak on her mantel offered ample testimony to her concern for or involvement in the field. She was usually disparaging of "people who just push buttons and call it art."

The newspaper was another way to stimulate Barnes. She hadn't read one regularly for years; there is every possibility that she never read one regularly at all. She had only momentary interest in politics, sports, business, or other topics. Literary reviews, gossip, and entertainment interested her more. Yet if I had a *New York Post* with a particularly lurid headline sticking out of my bag, she'd want it, become suitably outraged, and then grumble as she turned the first dozen or so pages. I often wondered how she might react to the *National Enquirer*, but never tested her with that. A lurid headline would distract her from pain or the inability to be creative and would always stimulate the one faculty that time never diminished: her conversation.

This may always have been Barnes's greatest talent. She was intelligent, perceptive, witty, very quick, and articulate. She had a forceful delivery and had once been proud of her "dominant voice." Now she was ashamed of it; emphysema had weakened it, and in her mind she wheezed and coughed all the time. These problems did exist but not to the degree she imagined; her voice was still firm and resolute. I tried very often to convince her to make some recordings of her best work, but with no success. I owned a sophisticated recording studio and could easily have made state-of-the-art recordings in her room, but she was unable to comprehend the recording process. In her mind recording had hardly advanced since the Edison cylinder. I would sit there day after day listening to her discuss various subjects, clearly and intelligently.

She read *Nightwood* or her poems, but try as I might she'd never agree to record them. I regret this very much. I was so persistent that she often accused me of secretly recording her. It would have been easy to accomplish, but I never did except on a single occasion—as I was to learn later—on my telephone answering machine. I discovered she had once made a short recording on a small cassette recorder years before I knew her. It may well have been the poor quality of this recording that prevented her from doing a professional recording of her works.

We talked and talked; there was scarcely a subject we didn't cover. Perhaps if Barnes had been able to comprehend the recording process she might have produced more varied work. Spontaneous in speech, she was deliberate in her writing. Every syllable was carefully structured. Yet when she spoke she was a superb conversationalist. Her writing was so consciously complicated that one often needed a dictionary close at hand to know what she was writing about. She always had one at the ready and it was apparent in every line.

If Barnes had possessed the ability to liberate her spontaneity and make use of it, she might have been less self-centered and able to get outside herself more often, to explore something other than her family and close circle of friends. It might have infused her writing with some measure of wit, an element sorely lacking in almost everything she attempted after *Ladies Almanack*. Had she recorded her thoughts she might have achieved greater breadth in her work. She was most perceptive in a wide range of subjects, but never wrote about most of the matters she discussed with me, always preferring to return to the same gloomy subjects. There is always the possibility, of course, that she felt that subjects other than death, lost love, infidelity, and a miserable family were unworthy of serious literature, or perhaps she eventually became too insecure to work outside the range she had established for herself in the 1920s.

Another possibility may have been laziness. It is after all much easier to talk than to write. Her meager output between the publication of *Nightwood* and her death forty-seven years later may just have been the result of being undisciplined and tending toward idleness. She did have continuing financial difficulties, few friends, and constant illnesses, but many lesser intellects have overcome such obstacles. Barnes was, in many ways, a towering figure, flawed to be sure but capable of keen insight and creativity. She knew she had wasted her time, spoke of it constantly, and was fond of quoting T. S. Eliot who had once remarked that it was true, she had wasted much of her time, but she should also consider how marvelous she had been when not wasting it. To me, this was begging the question, but Barnes enjoyed begging it and perpetuating the mystery. She often spoke of being marvelous. It was one of her favorite words and undoubtedly the way she always wanted to be. It was also her crutch. If she couldn't be marvelous she didn't want to be anything at all, except perhaps left alone. It was an easy way out; if a glorious phrase was not immediately forthcoming, it was because it was so difficult to be marvelous very often. Remove the paper from the typewriter and put the pencil down. She then had few choices for activity. She could read, listen to the radio, or talk with someone. There were few books on her shelves published after 1960 when I arrived, and New York AM radio is not particularly uplifting. There were fewer and fewer people to talk with as years went by; and by 1978 there was almost no one.

I knew Barnes for about three years and during this time was never aware of her reading any book from cover to cover—her limited vision prevented it—and she always listened to the same radio station. Conversation was what engaged her mind in her last years. Most of the time I was with her we simply talked, and she *was* usually marvelous. Even when choked with coughing fits and racked with pain, she was fascinating, a constant source of amazement. This is the way it was when I knew her, and it had probably been so for years. Her forté was her conversation—spontaneous, witty, and forceful conversation—on a soapbox raging against all the real and imagined injustices that bedeviled mankind in general and Miss Barnes in particular. Pontificating on anything and everything: the tiny bed was her Hyde Park corner and I was an assembled crowd of one. If she had only chosen to make more use of this aspect of her talent, she would have been marvelous more often than she could ever have dreamed possible.

Barnes loved to talk about people and ideas, but people were her favorite: it was far easier to be witty about them than about ideas. She often made the point she'd met "everybody" at least once; everybody meant literary folk and the people with whom they associated, those active from the time Barnes reached New York to the outbreak of World War II. When she was writing for newspapers and magazines, everybody included an assortment of celebrities as well. An accurate list of the people who filled her mind might be obtained by checking the index of each book written by Sylvia Beach, Malcolm Cowley, Margaret Anderson, Robert McAlmon, and others who were in New York and Paris in the time between the years 1910 and 1940. Select all the people listed, add her family and some celebrities, and Barnes's list of everybody would be complete. These were the people she remembered, who lived in the books that filled her shelves. With the exception of Dag Hammarskjold and some publishers, few people she considered of any consequence had entered her life after she moved to Patchin Place.

It may be that she didn't even consider her publishers worthwhile; she rarely met with them and usually referred to them as her "printers." I don't know whether she ever met James Laughlin of New Directions; she never mentioned him. I know she never met Roger Straus, though she did speak with him on the telephone when he was preparing the reissue of *Selected Works*; and she loved to tell one story about a meeting with his associate Robert Giroux, who had worked with her on the first version of *Selected Works*. They had several meetings while organizing the material and once the book was printed, Giroux called on Barnes with an armful of books for her to autograph. She was incensed and asked him to leave. She claims he left in such a hurry that the books were left behind, whereupon she gathered them up and threw them down the stairs after him.

There was a time when a book of memoirs by Barnes might have caused a sensation. She bragged that she had been offered millions for her memoirs but never accepted any offers: She was disinclined, she said, to tell stories about her friends. She meant she didn't want to tell stories about them in print, but she could talk about them from morning to night and she did so. When Barnes was at her best, her tiny room in Patchin Place became a time machine that she had flown in for four decades. Her room had been devoid of listeners for years; I was a fresh face and she knew I liked to listen.

In our hundreds of meetings the same stories were often repeated many times, stories of the people and events closest to her or perhaps of those she wanted me to remember.

Her relationship with these people, and how she viewed their place in history, were enlightening. The days of her youth, at least after she left home, would come alive in an optimistic way. She was never maudlin, never pined for days long gone. She talked of her friends in a cheerful way, almost as if they were alive and well, living next door. The times of her greatest successes and the spirit of those times glowed as she talked with her caustic wit and apparently precise memory. Joyce, Eliot, Crane, Pound, O'Neill, McAlmon, Wilson, Millay, Ford, Fitzgerald, and Boyle were the figures she recalled most frequently. Of later associates, such as Beckett, Dylan Thomas, Charles Henri Ford, Cummings, Witter Bynner, and Marianne Moore, she talked occasionally. Those on the periphery of her "literary" crowd were Peggy Guggenheim (and her children), Berenice Abbott, Mary Reynolds, Baroness Elsa von Freytag-Loringhoven, Natalie Barney, Margaret Anderson, Mina Loy, Mary Butts, Janet Flanner, Solita Solerno, Tommy Earp, and Emily Coleman. Cocteau, Duchamp, Man Ray, Steiglitz, O'Keeffe, and Chaplin also turned up, with hundreds of others whom she had met once or twice. The people to whom she had been very close were constantly in her thoughts, particularly Thelma Wood and Franz "Putzi" Hanfstaengl. Courtenay Lemon, to whom she was once ostensibly married, rarely surfaced; nor did her first lost love, Mary Pyne, then dead nearly sixty years. Charles Edison, the son of the noted inventor, was spoken of more often than Lemon or Pyne.

She often said that if there was anything I wanted to know about her family, I should simply read her books. When I told her I had read all her books and that was quite enough, she roared with laughter. She did, however, speak of her family frequently, usually negatively, except for her mother and grandmother. Saxon, a younger brother, still alive, she spoke of often: also usually negatively. A half-brother, Duane, was also alive and lived somewhere in the vicinity of Philadelphia. Though she was less inclined to talk about him, she seemed to be more understanding. In general, just as her family had been the source of much of her writing, it remained the source of much of her rage. Her brother Saxon was the family member most often raged against because he was still "meddling" in her business, and "no more than a telephone call away."

Djuna Barnes was stern and could be extremely harsh in the years I knew her, but she had very affectionate, tender feelings for a small number of people, two of them still living. In her conversations with me her fondest and most frequent recollections were of four male friends: Putzi Hanfstaengl, T. S. Eliot, Dag Hammarskjold—all long dead—and Silas Glossop, then still living in England. An equal number of female friends figured regularly in her memories: Emily Coleman, Peggy Guggenheim, Thelma Wood, of course—all dead—and Phyllis Jones, still alive and, like Silas Glossop, living in England.

Barnes remembered these eight individuals with longing and what seemed to be genuine affection. That she was understanding of Wood was amazing. It seemed she had actually come to a point in her life when she could pity this obviously pitiful woman.

Barnes said often, "I like to be with men a great deal more than I like to be with women, but I don't really want to be with either!" She offered variations on this theme innumerable times, but there were, indeed, the memories of a few men that meant a great deal.

Putzi Hanfstaengl had been close to her and remained so in memory. He was German, and they had a love affair as early as 1914, when he was in the U.S. and, according to Barnes, it was a serious relationship. She once said, "I was engaged to Putzi for about twelve hours," and laughingly added, "and that was long enough! What would I have done with all those German children?" She knew him for at least sixty years; I never asked her when Hanfstaengl died, but when cleaning out her back room I found a beautiful calendar he had sent her in 1974. It was still rolled up as it had arrived with a fine printed label from Hanfstaengl attached. He lived in Munich and in a very shaky hand had addressed the package to Djuna Barnes, Patchin Place, Greenwich Village, New York City. Barnes, in an equally shaky hand had added the date, 1974. She told me he had tried to give her modest sums of money primarily during her hard times in the 1940s and 1950s, but she had always refused it. Usually, after talking about this she would say, "He saved my life twice, first in the airplane and then when he didn't marry me. It was not necessary for him to save me any more." The allusion to the airplane had to do with a time in the teens when Barnes was desperate to fly and made arrangements to go up in an aircraft Hanfstaengl regarded as unsafe. After much arguing he prevailed; the aircraft went up with a few passengers, but without Barnes, and promptly crashed, killing everyone aboard. Barnes no longer had an urgent desire to fly.

Hanfstaengl apparently was in the good graces of the Nazi leadership for a few years. Barnes often told how she ran into Putzi in Berlin shortly after Adolph Hitler's abortive 1923 "Beer Hall Putsch." Putzi was looked upon favorably by the budding socio-path, having lent the Nazi Party one thousand dollars in that year. He told Barnes he was willing to arrange an interview for her with Hitler, who was in hiding, but he wanted two dollars a word because he was flat broke. She claims she wired *McCall's* magazine, for whom she was a stringer, and requested the funds, but the magazine evidenced a total lack of interest. She always felt it was a great failure on her part not to have tried harder to arrange that interview. Had she done so, she said she would have discovered Hitler's monstrous intentions and turned him in, no matter how much it might have hurt her former lover. It was not serious fantasy: she would always add with a sly smile, "I could have prevented World War II."

Actually, Hanfstaengl was a sometime-Nazi who played the piano and clowned for Hitler. He cared for Barnes very much. Despite his obvious political failings, despite the bouts in which he'd twist Barnes's arm until she'd agree to try to learn German, she did care for him. She never mentioned any personal contact with him after he renounced Hitler and fled to the U.S., but it seemed more than likely that they did meet. The only picture with any color in her apartment was a postcard, "Violets" by Dürer. It was on the corner of the bureau and she never moved it in all the time I knew her. It had probably been there for years before I arrived. It was from Putzi.

Her closest literary friend was T. S. Eliot, whom she regarded highly both as a person and a writer. She summed up her feeling about his writing simply: "I'm not so fond of his poetry but I care for his criticism a great deal." This is hardly surprising. Eliot was an early booster of hers; his introductory essay for *Nightwood* gave the work a new lease on life at a time when it was sorely needed, both by its author and its publisher. His comments meant much to her; she looked to him for guidance, criticism, and advice. After *Ryder* was reissued in 1979 and she became increasingly annoyed with the short introduction I'd written for it (with her help and blessing), she would look at me sternly and say, "Only Tom Eliot had my permission to write something in one of my books!" I would always change the subject, knowing that any conversation on that score had no chance.

She missed Eliot a great deal; it was as if there was no one left with whom she could discuss literary matters on an equal footing, and besides he was the ranking man of letters who held her work in high regard. Even though the world rejected *The Antiphon*, Eliot had praised the play's last act, so that in her mind it was a success. It was never clear whether she regarded Eliot as a finer critic than her other primary booster, Edwin Muir, but Eliot's greater reputation and influence was far more important to her. I suspect that she admired Eliot more as a literary figure and as her publisher; Eliot's admiration of Barnes was more personal. About the last time she was with him, at a luncheon in New York, she said, "He sat there with his face in his plate; he knew it was all over. His last words to me were, 'Goodbye my darling.'" Somehow I doubt if these would have been Barnes's last words to Eliot, but I may be wrong.

While organizing Barnes's poems and papers I came upon a small folder of letters and extracts of letters from Eliot; by extracts I mean that Barnes had cut out portions of his letters and kept them, separate from the regular correspondence file. I was on the floor under her desk, when I told her I'd found what seemed to be a batch of letters from Eliot; she became excited and asked to see them immediately. I handed the folder to her and after looking at it carefully, she said this small folder had been misplaced for years and it was a joy to have it back, safely in her hands. Under no circumstances was anyone to know what was in these letters, and she had worried it might have been included in the papers that went to the McKeldin Library. She said she should probably destroy them, but to the best of my knowledge she never did. Though she often spoke of the folder, she never revealed its contents. She often repeated her desire to destroy the letters, but could never summon the courage to do so.

Dag Hammarskjold was part of Barnes's life for a short while, but the timing and the intensity of their intellectual relationship left a lasting impression on her. She was proud that, at a time when little else in her life seemed optimistic, the "king of the world," as she called him, had not only praised *Nightwood*, but had taken time to translate *The Antiphon*, had arranged for its production in Stockholm, and wished to continue to meet with her as well. She said when he was killed in the then Congo it had taken something out of her; if he hadn't perished, her old age might have been very different.

All the truly "rare" books in Barnes's possession had been turned over to the McKeldin Library in the early 1970s; those remaining were originally slated to be given to the Salvation Army until I convinced her that this was a poor decision. Hammarskjold's book was the exception; it was almost as important as Eliot's letters, and also kept close at hand. Unlike the letters, however, it had to be included with all her papers at the library. I'd usually suggest that she send it to them immediately as she couldn't read Swedish and they would take care of it better than she, but she wanted to keep it near her. The cover of the book was falling off by 1981, and I have no idea of its condition when it was filed with her other papers, but it was certainly her most precious book just as Hammarskjold's friendship was precious. He was the last if not the only new acquaintance of stature who paid any attention to her after her self-imposed exile to Patchin Place. The translation and production of *The Antiphon* was, perhaps, her final triumph.

* * *

The fourth man was Silas Glossop, her only living male friend. Their friendship dated from the 1930s when Barnes lived in London; now Glossop was living in Penzance. Barnes was silent about him. There was a good deal of correspondence between the two in her files, but by 1979 the flow of letters had reduced to a trickle, the only private correspondence she maintained while I knew her. I typed almost every letter for her signature but on occasion she'd hand me one that she'd done herself. It was always to Glossop. Andrew Fields refers to him merely as "S" in his biography, *Djuna*; I have no firsthand knowledge of any of the events in the relationship between them except that on her part it was very caring. She often showed me a faded color snapshot of two children sitting in the foreground of one of her paintings (of a lady lounging on a couch). The painting was in Glossop's possession. She never made clear whether the children or grandchildren were his. In 1981 he was the only male, indeed the only person alive, with whom Barnes made an effort to stay in touch by letter, besides the few with whom she had some business concerning a book contract or an outrage, whether real or imagined.

Though she was generally more kindly disposed towards men than women, at least in conversation, she seemed to have had a wider circle of female friends. She was not, however, charitable to most of them, including the four most frequently discussed; in fact she often found fault with them as well.

I first heard of Emily Coleman while *Figures in an Alphabet* was being completed. Barnes had asked me to type yet another "final version" and surprisingly suggested that I type on a separate page a simple dedication to Emily Coleman, a name which had not come up in any conversation. When I asked who this person was and why the poem was to be dedicated to her, Barnes replied that Coleman had once been a dear friend who had died a few years before, and that "if it hadn't been for Emily, *Nightwood* might never have appeared." She felt it was an inadequate way to express her gratitude, but it was all of which she was then capable. That Barnes felt strongly enough about her to dedicate a book to her, no matter how trivial a book, indicated great affection.

Peggy Guggenheim was another matter. Barnes talked of her frequently with admiration, annoyance, gratitude, and mock outrage, for Guggenheim may well have been the most important person in her life, and Barnes knew it all too well. If it had not been for the monthly stipend of three hundred dollars from Guggenheim, she might have starved. I don't know when Guggenheim began to provide this modest income, but by the time I arrived on the scene it had been coming in regularly for many years. After Guggenheim's death, her son, Sinbad Vail, made certain the allowance was maintained, although it was shifted to a quarterly basis. Barnes was concerned about its continuing and was greatly relieved when the first check arrived. I tried to convince her that she really didn't need it anymore. Her finances were sufficiently in order that thirty-six hundred dollars a year made no particular difference. But this small amount had meant so much for so long that she honestly believed she couldn't get along without it. I, too, was relieved when the first check arrived because she then ceased to worry about it.

Guggenheim had been part of Barnes's life for many years, but Barnes's part in Guggenheim's was of a much lesser degree. The two had not been close for some time. Barnes never said when they had last seen one another, but it must have been at least twenty years, perhaps about the time Guggenheim gave her the old portable typewriter she used for all her work. There were a number of letters from her patron in the second collection of correspondence sold to the McKeldin Library as well as many postcards, dating from the 1920s through the 1950s. Barnes saved these postcards with hundreds of others to and from her various relatives. It was always a puzzle to me why she had hidden away so many postcards that she had sent from Europe to her mother and brothers. She transported them about Europe, finally storing them in the back room at Patchin Place. Anything associated with Guggenheim was retained: letters, postcards, books, memories.

Guggenheim went public in print the way Barnes went public in private conversation, speaking often of the lies and excesses in Guggenheim's memoirs and how outraged she was by her various books. It was a mock outrage, a pose against presumed impropriety. Barnes claimed she once challenged Guggenheim's remarks, saying, "How can you say such things about people when your own sister threw her children off the roof?" Guggenheim apparently replied it was not good manners to discuss "family" in print. This comment should have caused a strong reaction in Barnes; family was almost the only subject she ever discussed in print, but she never revealed her reply to Guggenheim. She was proud to point out, however, that she once forced Guggenheim to eliminate from one of her early memoirs a particularly lurid section dealing with Marcel Duchamp. Barnes convinced her that if the text remained as originally written, Mary Reynolds, who was then supporting Duchamp, would probably throw him out and he'd starve. The section was removed.

The Guggenheim memoirs fascinated her. When the final volume appeared, shortly after the death of her long absent friend, Barnes could not look at it quickly enough. She expressed annoyance that there was "so much screwing, as if that mattered at all," but was greatly concerned about allegations that *Nightwood* had been written at Guggenheim's residence in Hayford Hall, England, and that it had been written in a very short time. "How could she write such things? You don't write *Nightwood* in a month!" While she raged she was checking to see how many times she was listed in the index.

Guggenheim provided Barnes with financial support, lodging, many carefree days, and once, in the early 1940s, a show at her gallery, "Art of This Century." (Barnes was always annoyed that she wasn't included in Guggenheim's private collection.) The most visible gesture by Barnes in return was the dedication of *Nightwood*, shared equally by Guggenheim and the then-dead critic, John Holms. Considering Barnes's view of *Nightwood*, it may well be she regarded herself the more giving in the relationship.

Besides her mother, Thelma Wood was probably the most important woman in Barnes's life from the early 1920s until Wood's death in 1970. Long before I met Barnes I was aware only of the outlines of the relationship. It was not a secret. I had read *Nightwood* and was well acquainted with Berenice Abbott, who sometimes spoke about it, but I never brought Wood into conversation with Barnes; I felt it would have been impolite. She was not shy, however, in discussing her old lover. It began when she decided to show me an old scrapbook she had kept in the 1920s and 1930s.

It was full of hundreds of snapshots, in some instances formal, posed photographs. Almost all the snapshots were of Thelma Wood; any impartial observer would probably conclude the album was about Wood. She was pictured everywhere: on the beach, in an automobile, on a balcony, in almost every possible pose and circumstance. The photographs ended in the mid-1930s; at least this was the date in the notations. It was clear that Barnes's relationship with Wood had begun in the early 1920s, probably in Berlin, continued passionately until sometime in 1928, and then bumped along in fits and starts until near the middle of the next decade, a short while longer than some suggest. I don't know when it came to an end and never asked her. She spoke of Wood a great deal, usually repeating the same things over and over, making the point that she wasn't a lesbian because she loved Thelma Wood. I had known her but a few weeks when she recounted the first stories about Wood resembling her grandmother who had protected her from her father. She repeated it often; she wanted to make certain I remembered it.

She spoke of Wood in a friendly though not overly compassionate way. Many of the dusty, long unopened books on Barnes's shelves had once belonged to Wood; at least her name was written in many, and Barnes had retained one of her silverpoint drawings, a large study of a ferocious bull. It was buried at the back of her closet, kept all those years. She often repeated the story of how she had written *Ladies Almanack* at Wood's bedside, while she was recovering from some ailment. She once told me the story on the afternoon of New Year's Eve, and when she finished it I asked if there was anything I could get for her to help her manage through the evening, which I knew would be another long, lonely night, interrupted by horns and fireworks. She replied she needed nothing but recalled that she and Thelma had once "promised to think of one another when we heard the New Year's bells." I had lived in Greenwich Village for many years; I couldn't remember a New Year's bell, but perhaps Barnes was able to find one on her trusty antique radio and remember just the same. It probably pained her that when Wood was old, alcoholic, bloated, dying, and forgotten, she was unable to do anything but be in touch by telephone. The seemingly austere Barnes would probably have welcomed something more than a voice at the end of a telephone. I'm certain she remembered Thelma Wood far more frequently than on New Year's Eve.

* * *

About Phyllis Jones I know little other than that she was at the time (1980–81) about the same age as Barnes and living alone in England. She had apparently performed secretarial-type chores for Barnes in the 1930s. Though there had been minimal correspondence between them over the years, Barnes was concerned about her old friend's welfare. She spoke of Jones glowingly as a decent, kindly woman who had been understanding and of great help and, at this time of presumed need, she wanted to make a small donation toward her well being.

Barnes was aware that she was no longer destitute. The sale of her books and papers, the licensing of rights to her books, and proper investment of her money had increased her worth considerably. She once told me it was very important when one was old to have money, to enable one to give help to friends or leave it to someone in a will. She wished to remember Jones while she was alive, and modest amounts of money were withdrawn twice, converted to pounds, and dispatched to England. This was the only instance when I witnessed Barnes making an outright gift of money to anyone. She was very frugal, with justification; she often told the story of being penniless and having slept on park benches more than once. From her standpoint the modest gifts to Jones were significant gestures.

She discussed many other people who happened to wander through her mind. There was rarely an unkind word for her favorites. Others, not in favor, made a mixed bag. People from the past mingled willy-nilly with the delivery boy; they were another matter, and her comments were random, often caustic, sometimes hilarious.

The poet/critic Edwin Muir was close to her heart. He was often in her memory and visible in a small frame on her mantel as "the only decent critic who really understood my work." Hart Crane was a "raging pansy." He was also a "good poet but not top-drawer." She wondered how much Janet Flanner really wrote. "I think she went out to parties and socialized while Solita (Solano) stayed home and wrote." She rarely mentioned Flanner; this one comment was made about the time she received the check for one thousand dollars from the Flanner estate. Poor Natalie Barney was dismissed as "an old lesbian and failed writer who came from a family that made a fortune in toilet seats. She tried to have me but she didn't, and it rather annoyed her." Barnes admitted she modeled Dame Musset (from *Nightwood*) on Barney but never gave her permission to say it in public. "She did give me money when I needed it and for that I'm grateful, but why should that silly girl be allowed to meet Proust and why did she lie about her age; she was ninety-six when she died, not ninety-four." Alfred Stieglitz wasn't that old, but "was an old pansy who wanted young girls around for the sake of his ego. He told that young girl he married [O'Keeffe] to put her sex drive into her painting."

She'd known Margaret Anderson forever but regarded her as a foolish woman. "She was always drinking perfume and toilet water, and that's why the Baroness put dogshit on her doorstep." That Anderson had printed a letter from Barnes in the final issue of *The Little Review* was "the height of impertinence." How dared she to do that when "I had personally spoken with a judge to keep her out of jail during the *Ulysses* affair?" Kay Boyle was "often a good writer but usually uneven. The best thing she ever did was to describe the death of her husband as a 'roaring death.'" Later she dismissed Boyle by saying, "I think she's running a rooming house somewhere these days." Mary Butts, a much less known writer, got off easier but in a more mysterious way. Barnes described her as a "good writer with too much of a sentimental flourish." Once she said of Butts, "I remember her with Ezra Pound, that apartment and all the black magic."

Pound was recalled in a charming fashion. "The first time I called on him he invited me to bed. Naturally I refused but he helped me find a place to live." Later, as I've said, she managed to visit Pound at St. Elizabeth's Hospital in Washington, D.C. She was proud that in the 1950s she was still able to "interview" someone and that "even Ezra talked to me. I went down to see him in Washington and he talked. I don't remember what he said, but he really did believe all that foolish poetry he wrote in the early days was good when he wrote it."

"Joyce used to read me *Finnegan's Wake*. I'm in it but I don't know exactly where, and I'll be damned if I'll go and look for it." She admired Joyce a great deal and never made a disparaging remark about him. She held his writing in the highest regard; that she didn't think he was much of a poet is inconsequential. She was proud she had refused all overtures from the James Joyce Society (doubtless the one that would meet regularly at the Gotham Book Mart) to say anything about Joyce or the manuscript. "I showed them that some of us have enough sense to keep quiet." She was not quiet in describing how she had to sell the manuscript "for one hundred dollars or so when I was destitute."

Samuel Beckett "was just a man who pretended to be Joyce's secretary." It's a puzzle why Barnes chose to be so hard on Beckett. They corresponded a good deal; his letters were judged the most valuable when the second half of her papers were sold. When I found the folder of letters from him, she said they had not only corresponded, but he had also given her some money from his *Waiting for Godot* royalties in the 1950s. She said she was desperate, and grateful to have it, but at the end of her life she was hard on her old friend. She once asked me to buy a book, any current book I might buy for myself, bring it by, and then read her a few pages. I chose a new Beckett book, *Company*. The next day I called on Barnes and told her I had a new book by her old friend, Samuel Beckett. She was interested in what he might be writing and asked if I'd read some to her. I began, and after about two paragraphs she stopped me and said, "Mr. O'Neal, everybody farts. Most people can stand the smell of their own farts but do not enjoy the farts of others. This is Sam Beckett farting." I put the book back in my bag and we both laughed.

London,
early
1920s

EMIL HOPPE

She never mentioned e. e. cummings, who had lived about one hundred feet away, and she had but one thing to say about Auden—that he had "a face like an elephant's ass." I never told her that other people were credited with the same remark; she thought it was her own. For Anais Nin, who also lived in Greenwich Village, Barnes had no use at all. She claimed Nin used to follow her about the Village, hoping to speak with her, but she'd managed to avoid her. She once remarked that Nin had written some "pornographic stories," and I told her they'd recently been published. She was eager to see them so I bought one for two dollars in a remainder shop and brought it to her. Upon reading a few pages she commented, "This is utter rubbish. It is badly written, not even good pornography." It is interesting that Nin did manage to visit Barnes in the early-to-mid 1950s. There is a brief description of Barnes's apartment in one of Nin's diaries. This description could have been written twenty-five years later. Nothing had changed except the calendar and the box in the closet where old calendars were kept; small $2^1/_4$-by $2^1/_2$-inch daily entry-desk affairs, each year tied at the corner with twine—a box full of one year after another where almost nothing changed from year to year except the number of calendars.

Dylan Thomas was known in various Village places in the same years. Barnes was wild about him and had been from the moment she heard him. She was certain he had the finest speaking voice in the English language and was proud he'd reviewed *Nightwood* favorably when it was first issued in England. She was distressed, however, when the writer of a review of Thomas's comments couldn't understand how he could enjoy *Nightwood*, since he'd just been married. This made no sense to Barnes and every time Thomas came up in conversation she'd mention that this puzzled her, as did the poor sales of his reading of a selection from *Nightwood* on a Caedmon record. The royalties were always modest, never more than twenty dollars a year, but the humiliation of poor sales was offset by his glorious voice. She was pleased to have been present at his first reading of *Under Milk Wood* at the YMHA and would often sigh and recall, "That boy had a voice." On other occasions when she was on a tear, raging against all the sexually indulgent, she'd say, "All those dreadful buggers were after him all the time. I'm sure they got him!"

Berenice Abbott figured in many of our conversations; Barnes was well aware that Abbott was a good friend of mine, that we worked closely together. Of course, Barnes had known her since 1918, half a century longer than I, and we viewed the lady from a very different perspective. She inquired about Abbott frequently, but it was clear she didn't really have a caring interest; in her mind Abbott was still an eighteen-year-old girl trying to find herself. That she had become an artist who, in 1980, was probably far more well-known and respected than Djuna Barnes was an annoyance. If Abbott was having an exhibition or was interviewed in a newspaper, she'd evidence interest, but when I'd tell her about a particular incident she'd shake her head, look at me, and say, "I know about that little number." I don't know what she meant, but Abbott was the only person she ever referred to as a "little number." It also caused her much concern that Abbott was so well-paid for her work, "after all, she just pushes a button and the camera does the rest." When I told her our advance for *Berenice Abbott— American Photographer* was twenty-five thousand dollars, I thought she might fall out of bed. She exclaimed, "I can't stand it. I simply can't stand it." She used this phrase only on those occasions that were, in her opinion, utterly outrageous. She would shake her head in disbelief. How could a photograph, which to her any fool could take and have processed at the drug store, be worth anything? How could a book of photographs be worth an advance ten times as much as Farrar Straus was willing to pay for the reissue of *Selected Works?* We discussed this many times, but no matter what I might say nothing would dispel her notion that there was no difference between a snapshot and a well-printed, well-organized photo-graph. She had no basis for understanding such a thing even if she did once recognize the merit of a Walker Evans photograph. She never had such an understanding of Abbott; it was probably just outright jealousy, one of the few blind spots I ever encountered in her.

An interesting incident involving Barnes and Abbott, and re-vealing a good deal about Barnes, had its origin in the early 1950s when Abbott was still living on Commerce Street in Greenwich Village. Barnes had once told me that Abbott had photographed her in the 1950s, but it was "against my will." She added, "That little number was always full of tricks and one day when I went to visit her, she snapped her camera just as I walked through the door." I recalled having seen some negatives in Abbott's file marked "Djuna Barnes" and decided the next time I was in Maine visiting, I'd ask about them and make some prints. A few months later I had occasion to ask, and Abbott remembered the day well; she'd made many exposures, but it was not a successful session, and she'd never printed most of the negatives. If I wanted to make up some contact sheets to see the results, it was all right with her.

I sorted the negatives, then made some contact sheets and a few prints (see Appendix I, p. 201). Abbott was correct; the session was not successful, but only from a technical standpoint. Most of the negatives were so dense they required six minute exposures. A few of the images were very good. What was most revealing appeared to be the circumstances of the session. On the one hand Barnes was telling me "that little number tricked me," and on the other I saw photographs of Barnes coming through the door at least half a dozen times wearing different arrangements of clothing. The pho-tographs were in sequence; they were not made on different days, and there were photographs posed as well as those of her coming through the door. One had even been used in the past; the book about Barnes by Louis Kannenstine featured one on the cover. Nonetheless, here was Barnes telling me how she was tricked when it was clearly not the case. All of us engage in selective memory in one degree or another to suit our own purposes, but in this instance the selector was obviously tripped up. I never told Barnes what I had discovered; there was no purpose to be served in doing so.

The selective memory worked both ways. Abbott had photographed Barnes twice in the 1920s. One was a profile which has been used on various dust jackets; the other, the less familiar front view, has usually been reserved for photography shows and books about Abbott. Barnes always claimed she was dressed by Abbott in the elaborate turban and elegant clothes. Abbott, on the other hand, claimed that Barnes arrived that way; clothes and an elegant appearance were terribly important to her. The three-quarter view, reproduced here (p. 103), is taken from a unique print; the negative no longer exists and was presumably destroyed.

There were a few strains between the two, but after all this time they were still very good old friends. They had known one another for over sixty years and had many friends and memories in common. They had once shared an apartment during Abbott's first days in New York, when Barnes was ostensibly married to Courtnay Lemon, and they shared memories of Paris, Berlin, and probably much more. A photograph of Abbott with Thelma Wood in 1921 perhaps tells part of the story. One day we were discussing the book I was working on and Barnes said, "Well, I gave Berenice the extra e in her name and she gave me Thelma. I don't know who made out better." There is no question in my mind; Abbott kept the extra e for many years longer than Barnes kept Wood, and removed herself from the conflict that seemed to surround this woman. She didn't have to endure the heartache or the difficulties caused by Wood. Yet, in 1970, it was Abbott who was able to visit the dying Wood, and when Barnes died in 1982, the two old friends had been in touch only by telephone for years and even the calls were rare.

The Baroness Elsa von Freytag-Loringhoven was another wildly eccentric woman shared by Barnes and Abbott, at least on an intellectual level. Abbott mentioned her to me some while before I knew Barnes, but eventually I found myself in the middle of conflicting interests, opinions, and memories. Barnes had known Baroness Elsa earlier but it was Abbott who was closest to her. The young and impressionable Abbott was in awe of the carefree sense of abandon that characterized the life of the Baroness. She loved her poems, her drawings, almost everything about her. Abbott has often said that she was greatly influenced in her younger years by this woman, only avoiding the obvious self-destructive aspects of her character. Barnes, however, viewed her from a distance, particularly when she was behaving in an outrageous way or depositing dogshit on Margaret Anderson's doorstep. As time passed all three eventually wound up in Europe; they overlapped for a moment in Berlin, and then finally in Paris. Abbott and the Baroness had a falling out over a man and then two things happened; Abbott, in her own words, "turns the Baroness over to Barnes for safekeeping," and in a fit of rage the Baroness stole a portrait she had made of Abbott. As the peculiarly titled Pole became stranger and stranger, Barnes tried to aid her with her poetry and writing, and the Baroness came to believe that Djuna Barnes would see to the publication of her poetry. Barnes received lengthy, impassioned letters, a poor-box was robbed, the contents were forwarded to Barnes, and then, after a series of misadventures, the Baroness accidentally killed herself, leaving her entire literary estate to the bewildered Barnes.

It is doubtful that Barnes encouraged the Baroness to leave her literary legacy in her care. In fact, Barnes often said it would have been more appropriate if the papers had been left to Abbott. But through a twist of fate Barnes found herself responsible for a mass of poems, prose, drawings, and decorated pages. A few had already been typed by Barnes and Peggy Guggenheim, from the original manuscripts, but for the most part the pages were unorganized. Barnes probably looked on the situation in horror, but managed to arrange for a tribute to appear in *transition*, with a short statement by herself and a selection of prose and poems by the Baroness. Then silence. Nothing appeared for over fifty years.

In early 1979 Barnes asked me to attempt to sort out the Baroness's poems and arrange for their publication. A few months later I made a trip to the McKeldin Library and, armed with an appropriate note from Barnes, reviewed all the prose and poems and made copies of almost everything in the file. Shortly there after, Barnes gave me a thin folder that she said contained every- thing she had relating to the Baroness. She was emphatic; fifty years earlier she had told her friend her poems would be published. She had neglected her obligation until now and it was weighing heavily on her mind. The poems had to be published.

The thin folder Barnes gave me contained a few photographs, a letter, a very fragile color drawing, and a number of manuscript pages, apparently typed by Barnes herself. This was, apparently, the project with which she'd busied herself when the first draft of *Nightwood* (*Bow Down*) was complete. I saw a thinly fictionalized account of the Baroness's life, and in reading these pages two things became immediately apparent; the project did not go well, and Barnes's work habits in the early 1930s were not different from

1979. She had started the project in 1932 and then started again and again, always beginning from page one. Even then it seemed she had difficulty in beginning a story, poem, or in this case a loosely autobiographical novel, and continuing through to a conclusion. She would begin, type a number of pages, and stop. Then she would repeat the process with minor alterations. The project was never completed. It seems that no effort was ever made to do anything with the Baroness's poems. Barnes looked upon the woman as a character, a source of material (which is hardly in dispute), rather than a poet of any significance. Barnes was making an effort to produce a booklength work outside the scope of her family, and it proved fruitless.

I transcribed as many of the poems as possible, typed them up, and showed them to Barnes. She was decidedly noncommittal, but urged me to do anything in my power to arrange for publication. She made no mention of her efforts in the 1930s, but did agree to do a short introduction to the book. This never happened, but arrangements were made for a book of poems to appear in 1987—sixty years after the Baroness's death. It was to include a large selection of poems, some prose, a few drawings, plus almost all the memorabilia in the folder Barnes had retained, as well as a nude photograph of Duchamp, Barnes, and the Baroness together in the 1920s. (Berenice Abbott had the negative for the photograph but says she did not take it.) Abbott did supply a wonderful photograph of her eccentric friend wearing a hatlike object that is most peculiar. The circumstances of this photograph are lost in time, but it apparently portrays "the real Baroness." It took over sixty years, but Barnes's obligation had finally been met.

Other names from the past were a constant part of her conversation. She would tell charming stories about all these assorted personalities. The stories were usually funny, made even more so by Barnes's natural wit and acerbic tongue. Many of her comments had serious sexual overtones; she always talked of lesbians, pansies, and buggers, never using the word homosexual. She rarely spoke of ordinary heterosexual activity other than to repeat over and over that "the motion was ridiculous but the feeling was sublime." Of the dozens of different people who would appear in her memory in a day, she would speak as though they were in the next room or as if she'd seen them the day before. She was deeply fascinating when she did this, and while the stories rambled I became a passenger with her in the time machine that usually landed somewhere in the 1920s.

No, she couldn't hit a spittoon from forty feet. It was that dreadful columnist Walter Winchell who had said so, but the honor in fact belonged to someone known affectionately as "Doris the Dope." Who was Doris? Barnes never revealed her identity but did say she let the story stick. She couldn't fight Winchell. She'd point proudly to the photograph of her walking along the street in Berlin with Chaplin and Jimmy Light. Of course, she'd known him long before that afternoon. In fact, Chaplin had once appeared in one of O'Neill's plays at the Provincetown Playhouse, with Light directing. He had a small, unannounced walk-on role two nights in a row and no one made anything of it. He just did it and was happy to have the experience. Jack Dempsey: she'd once interviewed him while he was champion. Jack Johnson had propositioned her, and pinched her as well, but Dempsey was well-behaved. He said he stayed away from women before a serious fight, that a woman could drain all his energy. When she asked how he abstained from sex for such a long time, he said he didn't and pointed towards a young man, saying, "What do you think I keep him around for?"

F. Scott Fitzgerald told her the entire story of Gatsby one night at Julius's before he had written a single word, and it was a good story. She had known Fitzgerald well but wished she had known him better. She wished she'd known Carl Van Vechten less; he photographed her once when she returned from Europe on one occasion, and all the portraits were "simply terrible. He made me look just like a nigger (p. 71)."

Then she'd remember Marsden Hartley with a sly smile, he'd once made a pass at Thelma and even though he was an old "pansy," he thought he'd follow up on his initial advance. He came to visit Wood at the apartment where she and Barnes lived, but as Hartley climbed the stairs, Barnes, unbeknownst to him, was lurking in the shadows ready to pounce on her presumed rival. As he reached the top of the stairs, Barnes leapt from her hiding place and hit him over the head with a large stick, sending him tumbling down the stairs. She laughed recalling how ridiculous he looked, but not as ridiculous as he would have looked in bed with Thelma.

Speaking of ridiculous, there was always Witter Bynner, "a perfectly horrible poet." Everything he wrote was a joke and he told her so. He wrote all his nonsense to bamboozle a lot of stuffy critics who thought they knew about modern literature. He laughed and laughed when they took his "poetry" seriously. He must still be laughing because some critics have still taken him seriously, and all his works have been recently republished.

Edmund Wilson was an old lecher; he once put his hand on her knee at the Brevoort and made what to her was an unseemly suggestion. Naturally she refused. He tried it again in Europe a year or so later and, naturally, she refused again. Wilson was not very pleasant after the second rejection.

She'd met Gurdjieff once and "knew he was an old fraud," but wanted to interview him just the same. He refused to let her draw a picture of him, so she walked out without the interview. The gunmen who were present when she interviewed Fanny Brice wouldn't let her walk out, but in this case she didn't care to. She interviewed André Gide when she first arrived in Europe, and he became a friend, but then became her enemy when he refused to write an introduction to the French edition of *Nightwood*. The "silly old pansy" was scandalized by its subject matter.

Back the machine would fly to the U.S. where she rarely saw e.e. cummings, though she did see his wife, who photographed her (p. 17). She did see Marianne Moore fairly often, didn't like her very much, but wasn't it amazing how much money she made playing the stock market? There was also "a silly writer" around town at the same time named Margaret Young who wrote "a dreadful book" called *Miss McIntosh My Darling*, which was a modest success. She'd always followed Barnes about, perhaps fighting for room on the sidewalk with Anais Nin, but with her literary success she bought some new shoes, a cape, and two diamonds. She was never seen again by Barnes, and thank goodness. And "how dare Howard Moss change one of my poems?" Of course she changed it back. Lillian Hellman? Why bother with her and that silly little scandal? She'd wonder if Henrietta Metcalf was happy in Connecticut, or poor Allan Ross MacDougall. She'd helped him with his literary cookbook. Charles Henri Ford? What a silly boy. He didn't "live" with her as he claimed. She gave him a room once and he served more or less as her houseboy when she was ill. He had been helpful, but he hadn't lived with her and wasn't it dreadful for him to say such a thing.

So the conversations went on, day after day: an oral index of the Paris literary expatriates and their associates. It was as good a memoir of the times as offered by any of those who chose to commit one to print. It is unfortunate, however, that in Barnes's case there were no readers, just one good listener who is able to recall but a fraction of all she said.

Barnes didn't discuss her family a great deal unless a circumstance developed that was a result of the recollection of some relative. Yet her comments about these few family members, living and dead, while not particularly important, were just as spirited as her remarks on the assorted celebrities she had known. She probably had more relatives than she let on; with all the brothers and half brothers floating about, she must have had many nieces and nephews, but they rarely surfaced in conversation other than one who was snooping about her papers in Maryland, trying to gather enough information to write a "dreadful little book." Another was, in her mind, an utter horror. She claimed this one had tried to kill one of her brothers. Living relatives turned up infrequently, and it's hardly surprising since only a brother and a half-brother were still alive.

Poor Saxon Barnes. He was a constant subject, under continual verbal bombardment by Barnes, primarily because he was an amateur sculptor who had innocently produced a bust of his sister. He was a telephone call away and forever "meddling" in Barnes's affairs. I'm certain he was never aware of his sister's rage every time the subject of the bust reared its ugly precast head.

Saxon wanted to have his work cast in bronze and given a place of honor at the McKeldin Library, along with all the Barnes papers. In the first place Barnes viewed the entire episode as her brother's meddling in her affairs but, more importantly, she hated the bust. He'd sent her some polaroid snapshots, a serious error on his part. She loved to throw them around the room, exclaiming, "Look at these! He made me look like a boy! I never looked like this! I don't want to ever look like this!" She was convinced that her brother, a successful banker, was secretly jealous of her. She was, after all, in *Who's Who*, and he was not.

Saxon Barnes then contacted the University of Maryland directly, suggesting they accept the bust and include it with the Barnes papers. More rage and fury. I tried to distance myself as far as possible from being trapped in the middle of a dispute that obviously went far deeper than disagreement over the work of a Sunday afternoon artist. As the photographs were hurled in my direction I'd gather them up, look at them seriously, and keep silent. Barnes's rage at this innocuous bust resembled her rage at all her other tormentors. It made little sense on the surface. The only ulterior motive her brother might have had, in my opinion, was to work out an arrangement whereby he could get someone else to pay for the casting. To me it seemed inconsequential. He was perfectly reasonable at the times I talked with him on the telephone and seemed to think of his sister often, forever sending her presents. She usually discarded them or in some instances returned them to him. This was not my concern, except that I was usually the messenger who delivered the goods to the post office. This situation led to a grand fight between Barnes and myself—the undoubtedly celebrated dressing gown scandal.

Saxon once sent his sister a pale blue nightgown/dressing gown. It would just not do; it was too long, too short, or overly embroidered but, whatever the difficulty, Barnes wanted it returned immediately. It was rewrapped and dispatched to Pennsylvania but it never reached Saxon Barnes. It was a crisis of gigantic proportions. Barnes was very upset. Were they stealing dressing gowns at the post office? Was Saxon misleading poor Miss Barnes in claiming it never arrived, just because he knew it would annoy her? Was Mr. O'Neal the culprit? Had he merely thrown the package in the first trash bin he encountered to avoid the lines at the post office, or was he planning to give the garment to his girlfriend? All these possibilities were raised by Barnes as the crisis continued. There was no solution, but she never let me forget it and she probably believed I had it all the time.

Paris,
1921

The inner working of the Barnes family was public knowledge up to a point; beyond that I reasoned the best I could do was to avoid what was not my business. I didn't ever want to be in the middle of anything with this band of egocentric people. As I reread her books and listened to Barnes, I came to appreciate more and more the simplicity of my being an only child. The relationships within the Barnes family were very complex; no one seemed to care about the others as people; they cared about each other because they were related, but as people, they were insignificant, or rivals. Barnes told me that in seventeen years her brother, Saxon, had visited her one single time. She'd dwell on this painfully forever, usually ending by saying that even if this was the case, he was "family," and she couldn't forsake the family. Family was "part of you." She was terrified that one of her never-close family members might put her in a "snake pit," her favorite word for a nursing home. It was a justified fear; that was precisely what happened, and she would have died there if she hadn't been rescued by a benevolent non-relative.

It is unfair to say Barnes had no personal contact with other people. In the years I knew her, though the circle of acquaintances was not wide, there were a handful of people she saw regularly, some as frequently as once a week, some as rarely as three times a year. As I have indicated, the people who called on her infrequently were often subjected to violent criticism in their absence, criticism usually made to an often unprepared third party. When it was time for rage I would sit back, listen, and wait for her mood to change so we could discuss more interesting matters.

Barnes knew she was harsh with people, recognizing it herself as a serious flaw in her character. A kindly Haitian nurse, one of several who cared for Barnes, always did as well as she was able, but that she was not perfectly fluent in English aggravated Barnes a good deal. One day when the nurse had gone on an errand, Barnes began verbally abusing her to me. How could I have hired such a stupid woman, one who couldn't even speak English? She's lived here in the United States three years and still can't even speak English. What a stupid person—on and on. Finally, fed up with her invective, I suggested to Barnes that she was absolutely correct—that anyone who'd been in a country for three years and couldn't speak the language was obviously not very intelligent. I suggested that she should simply converse with her nurse in French. Having lived in Paris off and on for over a decade, and since she was certainly more intelligent than her nurse, she must be perfectly fluent in French. Barnes was startled; first she was shocked that I'd say such a thing, for I normally just reasoned with her quietly, but she also grasped how stupidly she was behaving. Though it did not stop her from criticizing this nurse, or any other, if her egg was not boiled properly or if she was a few minutes late, she did stop complaining about her lack of English.

If there is one characteristic of hers I remember most vividly, it is her constant criticism. It fell on almost everyone. It even appeared that the more she knew someone, the harder she was. I realized early on that she was pessimistic about every subject imaginable, but it always puzzled me why she was so uniformly critical of the few people around her who were usually guilty only of trying to be as kind and helpful as they were able. She repeated her belief that anyone would do her in for a little money again and again. She'd say someone would put a stick in her eye, and she believed it. She never revealed why she believed this to be the case or, more specifically, what had shaped her beliefs. One could surmise that the often bestial behavior of her father, the infidelity of Lemon, Wood, or whoever might have damaged her greatly, but it was difficult to understand how these could have been the only reasons.

I ultimately came to the conclusion that the criticism was a mask, an act to hide her real feelings, because I genuinely felt that her primary inclination, at least when she seriously considered a situation, was to be kind and understanding. She was harsh, critical, and often an old curdmugeon, but she was also capable of being unusually warm and sympathetic, at least to me. If this sounds confusing, it was and is; at the same time that she was cursing the delivery boy for bringing the wrong can of tomatoes, she'd be revealing great concern for someone she barely knew. A moment later, a minor transgression by someone trying to be kind would set her off. It made little sense to anyone victimized in that way.

I noted two people she never criticized; these people couldn't have been more dissimilar. Jussi Korzeniowski was a faithful person who assisted her with all kinds of domestic duties; and Maggie Condon, a woman I introduced to her, simply became her friend.

Condon lived in the Village, two blocks from Barnes. Bright, attractive, efficient, successful as a director of television commercials, she was not in awe of Barnes and was largely unconcerned with literature. Barnes, on the other hand, was fascinated with this obviously successful woman, looked forward to her visits, worried about her problems, and constantly inquired about her welfare. She even kept a portrait I'd made of her above her fireplace. It hid a bit of Edwin Muir. Condon was the only person I introduced to Barnes who managed to maintain a separate relationship, apart from me, and continued to see her when I voluntarily dropped out of Barnes's life. Of course Barnes constantly annoyed Condon, who often went on errands, shopping for lingerie or other items, and invariably would come back with something unsuitable. They'd argue, but Barnes enjoyed this woman's company more than almost anyone else in her last years. It is unfortunate that Barnes and I terminated our "arrangement" because it resulted in Condon's not being in touch with her as often. She visited her, but less and less often, just enough to keep up with events as Barnes's life wound down to its finish.

Jussi was loyal and kind, did as he was told, fixed her ceiling,

painted the room when the flood occurred upstairs, did the laundry
every week, and regularly came by to clean. He was hard at work
on Barnes's behalf long before I knew her and surely must have
continued to assist her until the day she died. He followed her
rules, cleaning the small room according to her wishes, and using
methods of which she approved. Accordingly, when Barnes drafted
her will in 1979 he was one of three individuals remembered—not
with a great deal, but remembered nonetheless. She was lucky to
have his services and probably knew it.

Jussi was once on holiday in Poland and she was very distressed
while he was away, fearing the awful communists might do something to him. I met with her the day he returned; he'd just left her
apartment when I arrived, and she showed me some religious
articles he'd purchased for her in his native land. She didn't
appreciate such items in her room, but said she planned to leave
them in view for a while so as not to offend her friend—extreme
sensitivity on one hand and incomprehensible outrage a moment
later.

Everyone else caught it at one time or another; my assistant simply
because he had a beard, people at my office if they failed to speak
deferentially, everyone at St. Martin's Press, the supposedly
drunken super of Patchin Place, the entire staff of Bigelow Pharmacy. One young man who once had seen Barnes regularly was also
regularly abused, once so thoroughly that he disappeared for about
six months. A young physical therapist who came to massage
Barnes's legs was dismissed as a drunk simply because at the end of
a long, tiring session she asked if she could have a drink from the
bottle of whiskey Barnes kept on the kitchen shelf. It was my
misfortune to have arranged for this masseuse to come by and
"break poor Miss Barnes's back." That all her suspicions about the

masseuse were false mattered not at all; Barnes was convinced the woman was a drunk and a crippler.

Fran McCullough, who had arranged for the Harper and Row edition of *Ladies Almanack*, thought very highly of Barnes, and did everything possible to assist her in obtaining a federal grant. She was accused by Barnes of forging her signature to a government form, simply because she didn't understand anything about how to apply for a grant. The controversy revolved around a clause at the bottom of one of the pages of a government form, which said the U.S. government reserved the right to publish excerpts from any work that the recipient of the grant might complete while making use of the funds. Barnes didn't understand the situation; to her the clause meant the government could publish anything she'd ever written, including *Nightwood*.

I tried to explain what it really meant, that the U.S. government might, underline might, wish to take an excerpt from a work she might complete in 1980 or 1981 to illustrate how a grant had assisted a noted author in her work. Since it was highly unlikely that anything would be published in those years, there was even less likelihood the U.S. government would want to use a line or two from *Creatures in an Alphabet*. Barnes, of course, refused to believe this and was convinced that since she had discovered this in the contract, she would never have signed the original application in the first place. In her mind, therefore, the application had been signed by someone other than herself. The fact that she was reading the clause concerning reproduction rights at the same time the award was made was irrelevant. She was certain someone else had done it and that was that. The situation became even more complicated when the money arrived. Now what could she do? If she accepted the money it meant to her mind that the U.S. government would undoubtedly begin gearing up to print *Nightwood* and everything else she had ever written. We argued for at least a month, and all the while she was accusing Fran McCullough of having forged her signature. She never changed her mind; to her dying day I'm certain she was convinced her name was forged, but eventually she relented and accepted the fifteen thousand dollar grant. I hoped that would be the end of it. It wasn't; the "forgery" cropped up again and again, and she spoke of the well-intentioned "suspect" in a most disparaging way. Her final position was that she had never applied for the grant in the first place; she simply dismissed the entire idea. But she kept the money.

Doctors were also a continuous source of frustration. They were all quacks and scoundrels looking to take her last penny. Barnes raged about Dr. Robert Coles, the man who had sufficient courage to attempt a lens implant operation, and many others, including a friend of mine, Dr. Albert Vollmer, a benevolent and skilled man. He'd repaired the teeth of many musicians to enable them to play their instruments, and I thought perhaps he could make a set of teeth for Barnes. I made him an offer he was unable to refuse: many free hours of recording time in my studio in exchange for just an attempt to make the dentures. He had to take all his equipment and his nurse/technician to Patchin Place, where he managed to do the job. No mean trick, for Barnes had almost nothing left in her mouth for him to work with. Yet she constantly complained about those dentures and never had a kind word for the doctor who had created them for her. If he'd not done the job, Barnes's diet would have consisted of mush for the last three years of her life.

Dr. Gustave Beck, her regular doctor, was as kind and tolerant a man as I have ever encountered and Barnes was fond of him, in her fashion. The previously noted short poem, "Imago," was created in his honor while she was confined to a hospital under his care. Yet, no matter how kind Dr. Beck might be, how thoughtful Dr. Vollmer, or how competent Dr. Coles, it was never enough. They were greedy duffers unable to make Miss Barnes well and able to do as she pleased, free of pain, able to see clearly and crack a walnut with her teeth. They just wanted her money, were ill-mannered with foul breath and worse. That she knew better than to criticize these doctors for her infirmities was beside the point; she did so nonetheless.

She must have had a grand time when she was a critic for the *Theater Guild Magazine* in the late 1920s and early 1930s. Since she no longer had a formal role as a critic, she elected to direct her energy in a less formal fashion: the man who "stole" her old, used paint roller; the people downstairs because their children left toys in the hall; the Greenwich Village Halloween Parade; the music at Trude Heller's (could she really hear that music at the corner of Ninth Street and Avenue of the Americas?); small children who wore "hobnail" boots as they played and clattered about on the Patchin Place "cobblestones"; and, of course, anyone who wanted to do anything with any of her written material. She acted out the part, criticizing everyone associated with her "papers"—Robert Wilson for having assisted Robert Beare in the initial removal, Robert Beare because he removed them to the McKeldin where she was certain "hoards of niggers were pawing through them all the time," Douglas Messerli, who was using the McKeldin papers to issue spurious editions of her old newspaper pieces, and, of course, Andrew Field, who was busy writing a biography that would undoubtedly dredge up pieces of the past that were unpleasant.

They were all villains, unseen, unspoken to, all perpetrating the worst offenses she could bring herself to imagine. "Why won't they let poor Miss Barnes alone!"

It is legitimate to ask how I put up with all this for the nearly three years in which I aided Barnes. I was also often the brunt of much of her criticism and, infrequently, rage as well, but for the most part, at least until 1981, her comments to me were offered in a kindly, often charitable fashion. It came down to my belief that her best work was important. It was a challenge to see what could be done to preserve it; she was a brilliant, fascinating woman; not always as much a terror as the foregoing might indicate.

Barnes was harsh and hateful but she knew it, often acting it out consciously, sometimes even in a joking, sarcastic way—an act she'd performed for so many years she seemed now to be a prisoner of the aura she had created. She would often rationalize it by saying she was "spontaneous"; she deliberately didn't see people because she was "too spontaneous." We argued about this with regard to Roger Straus. I thought it would be polite of her to ask him to call on her at the time he was reissuing *Selected Works*. She wouldn't hear of it. She said firmly, "The reason I see so few people is that I am too spontaneous and can make enemies very quickly. I can make more enemies in five minutes than you can make in five years."

The main reason that Barnes and I got along as well as we did for as long as we did was because I was then and remain today very calm in most situations. One must hit me with a stick to annoy me, and Barnes recognized it. No matter how vicious an attack she might make on someone, I'd continue whatever I was doing without changing my expression or attitude. She might declare a certain person an absolute shit, a liar, a thief, or worse; without any comment I'd continue the conversation in a rational way as if she'd said nothing out of the ordinary. This attitude heightened her anxiety until finally she gave me the name of "plate-face." She'd say things purposely to outrage me, but I wouldn't be outraged and she'd look at me sternly and say, "How can you just sit there!" Then she'd laugh and we'd continue with business as usual.

I had come to understand her moods. She had been injured; this and other problems caused her initial withdrawal and shaped her attitude toward everyone. She was also in constant physical pain and had to bear a good deal of mental anguish. All this was enough to create a person who, at eighty-seven, eighty-eight, and eighty-nine, could not accept even the smallest failing in someone. And her rules of civility and decorum were so severe and antiquated that no one, at least no one I knew, could ever measure up to them.

Barnes's critical nature and her intolerance were real, but often the reality didn't run very deep; the outrage didn't last. To be sure there were certain people who had utterly offended her, and she would not tolerate them in any way, but in most cases her caustic remarks and pompous attitude were for effect. She *was* spontaneous, and very amusing. She knew it and this was part of her art, the art of her conversation. She could be a horror to the delivery boy and criticize everyone in sight, but I recognized not only why she did it but why she had to behave that way. It was easy for me to understand because I saw it so often. It would have been impossible for anyone who saw her but once or twice a year to understand her, and equally incomprehensible to someone who was subjected to a single raging attack. How could it be otherwise? They had no basis for making a judgment.

Barnes was not very fond of the man who lived upstairs, the one whose plumbing had caused the flood in her apartment. She made unflattering remarks about his sexual habits, appearance, and so

forth. Yet she felt compelled to be kind to him when he appeared at
her door weeping after his mother died. I prefer to think of her that
way. She'd throw Robert Giroux out of her apartment with the
books tumbling down the stairs after him, but had he stumbled on
the stairway and injured himself, she would have been the first to
be alarmed and offer to assist. She was a complex woman, one
who'd call me a name one moment, recognize she was being
foolish, and then be kind in a flash. It was an act; I observed it as I'd
watch a play because I knew as soon as the act was over, reality
would probably return. This puzzled her; perhaps no one had ever
treated her in this fashion, but it was why we got along. I was
almost like an audience at a play witnessing Miss Djuna Barnes in
the art of raging conversation. Of course, it was also to her advan-
tage that I remain in the audience until the play came to an end
but, much to everyone's surprise, I walked out in the middle of the
last act.

Djuna &
Gorilla,
New York,
October
1913
or 14

*A*s 1980 inched towards 1981 it became increasingly evident that Barnes was incapable of ever undertaking any meaningful new work, or even editing and approving poems she'd written in the past. She was always frail but was now becoming obviously weaker. As this developed it is not surprising that she became progressively concerned with her failing health and rarely made her way to her desk. The desk was no more than eighteen inches from the end of her bed, but the distance lengthened with each day. As days crawled by she was less able even to make an attempt to work. When I'd arrive, normally in the late afternoon, it was rare to find her out of bed; eventually she chose not even to answer the door. She had given me a key to her apartment in early 1979, but usually she'd come to the door and let me in, unless she was ill. Now I'd knock and eventually I'd hear a faint "just let yourself in." I was terrified that one day there would be no answer. This happened only once.

My usual pattern was to call her late in the afternoon, when the most pressing daytime activity at the recording studio was over but before evening sessions began. One afternoon I telephoned and there was no answer. I rushed over to Patchin Place and banged on the door loudly. When there was no reply I cautiously opened the door and found Barnes in bed, breathing in what seemed to me a very labored way. I eventually managed to wake her; the problem was nothing more than having taken two sleeping pills instead of one, but it certainly made for some anxious moments. She promised to be more careful in the future.

Barnes completed no significant work in 1980 but, despite her weakened condition, her mind remained clear and in conversation she continued to be interesting and revealing. Many days I'd come by and as I entered the room she'd shout "Spring again!," a statement that could be taken on various levels. It was our standing joke. On the least complicated level, it meant she wasn't doing any work on her poetry, particularly on her favorite, *Rites of Spring*. The two words were also significant in a key phrase in *Ryder*. And her comment was also a mild reproach aimed squarely at me. She was always worried about my female companions, but no matter what the meaning, we'd laugh whenever she said "Spring Again!" for it was a signal that she was in a good mood, felt somewhat more energetic than usual, and wanted to talk, learn the news of the day, gossip about those souls locked in her memory, or give it to someone she felt to be currently deserving.

These conversations continued to range far and wide; people certainly were not the only topic. Almost everything came up at one time or another—sex, pride, religion, love, companionship, and even herself. She had serious opinions about almost every topic; some made sense and others didn't, but all usually revealed some aspect of her extraordinarily complex mentality.

She was ambivalent about sex, though she'd had serious and extended relationships with men and women for many years. A specialist would probably classify her as an ordinary bisexual female who was usually attracted to women in terms of long relationships. I don't pretend to understand what she thought of such matters, but I do know the positions she stated to me, always maintaining she was a prim and proper lady, one with very "old-fashioned" values. Yet her own behavior from the mid-teens to the late 1930s was hardly indicative of "old-fashioned" values. The average person in the United States in 1988 would probably find her sexual behavior in those years somewhat less than "old-fashioned." Perhaps Barnes felt she was virtuous simply because she was disinclined to discuss her relationships too publicly, except when they might pop up in the guise of literature.

Barnes was clearly homophobic; she was intolerant of and raged against "pansies," usually speaking of homosexual men in a disparaging fashion. She was equally derisive towards lesbians, claimed over and over that she hated them, and bridled when anyone suggested in print that she was one herself. I never witnessed anyone suggesting to Barnes that she was a lesbian, but if any of the young women I'd so carefully briefed broke the rules and suggested such a thing to her, it would have been disastrous. "Poor Miss Barnes" would have summoned all the energy at her command and pushed the offender out the door, perhaps whacking her on the head with her walking stick for good measure.

It seems clear that Barnes never came to grips with her own sexuality despite how much she seemed to have enjoyed rollicking sex in the past. There were periods of her life when she went through many men and women, apparently enjoying the pleasures of both, but in her old age she was prone to consider all sexual matters in a negative way. Her conversations indicated a general negative feeling towards all forms of male sexuality; this was also apparent in much of her later writings. She was forever talking of "little things," "worms," "a hanging piece of flesh," and "bulges." Eventually she directed much of her biting comments about sex toward me and often took exception to my female friends. One day she told me my schedule of work and play was more than anyone could possibly tolerate for more than a week or two, that I should stop producing so many records and drastically curtail my "womanizing." She said there was a perfect solution: she'd "put my little thing in a box of camphor," which would leave me more time for more serious matters. We both laughed at the suggestion: she more than I. There's little doubt that she meant it on some level; if I was late arriving, the blame was always shifted to a woman.

Another time a young man who edited a literary quarterly wrote Barnes, requesting permission to publish some of her old interviews. The letter was polite, the request reasonable, and a sample issue of his publication was included with the letter. She looked at the magazine very carefully, but it didn't take her long to discover a photograph of the editor, standing in a field wearing nothing but boots. She was outraged that such a person would even dare to write her a letter, let alone request permission to use her work. What a vile creature she presumed he was, standing there, wearing nothing but his boots and a stupid grin with his "little thing" exposed for all to see. She said, "All men think about is their 'little thing': who cares about them? Men's 'little thing' looks so stupid, just hanging there like a shriveled worm and who wants to look at a worm?" The letter was not answered. It gave her something to talk about for weeks.

Her homophobia was real and intense. It was puzzling to me why she made so much of it and was so firm in her conviction that she was not a lesbian. She loved Thelma Wood, but that didn't make her a lesbian—it didn't mean anything except she loved Thelma.

The subject of Barnes's sexual reputation arose often, sometimes for no reason, but in some instances because of an accusation someone might have made in print. I'd always try to express my attitude as "so what," it was irrelevant to me, and I felt she should feel the same way, but this was certainly not the case. In her mind there was a distinct stigma attached to being a lesbian, and her association with lesbianism weighed heavily on her: she thought it had tainted her reputation. This was why I briefed the young female writers and never told her about the many requests to interview her made to me from various lesbian organizations. She was sufficiently concerned about the topic to suggest she wouldn't have written *Nightwood* had she known what it would have brought down on her head. I knew she was serious. Once when I returned from a lengthy business trip, Barnes said I'd stayed away so long because one of our mutual friends had told me Miss Barnes was a lesbian. I wondered whether the publication of *Nightwood*, the attendant "widespread" belief that she was a lesbian, and the apparent social disgraces she felt caused her withdrawal into a nearly monastic existence. It seemed absurd, particularly after considering her lifestyle of the previous twenty-five years, but she made so much of how it had changed her life that in my mind it became a strong possibility.

Barnes recognized that what she had written in *Nightwood*, intentional or not, was regarded by many as a novel with a strong lesbian theme and was influential in ways she had probably never intended. This concerned her. It was acceptable for the strong literary qualities of the book to influence someone, but it was another matter if the book gave meaning or solace to young women, unknown to her, who were casting about in search of justification for their sexuality. "I don't want the responsibility of changing anyone's life," she would often say, "I don't want to make a lot of little lesbians!" She would tell me, "Girls used to kneel outside my door and beg to be let in and when they'd finally depart, they usually left flowers on the doorstep. One was so insistent, she just wouldn't leave, I had to telephone the police to take her away." This seemed somewhat drastic action to me, but it was perfectly acceptable to Barnes.

If Barnes was insecure about her sexuality, or sexual reputation, she was even more insecure with her old age, how she viewed herself, and how she presumed others viewed her. It was not just her infirmity that kept her hidden away in her room; it was her appearance. She was a very proud woman and in her eyes her looks began to deteriorate as she neared sixty. She once said, "I know what I look like. A hideous old woman. I look at myself and think 'this is not me.' How could it have come to this?" Berenice Abbott had photographed her twice, thirty years between the two sittings. The changes are obvious: she didn't age particularly well, but she wasn't hideous, merely old. To me she had great dignity; that she was stooped and wrinkled was merely reality, one I could easily accept. She remained a handsome woman, but Barnes couldn't accept her physical appearance any more than she could live with the "reputation" resulting from how some people chose to interpret *Nightwood*.

Barnes did what she could to make a difference, curling her hair, standing up as straight as possible to greet a stranger, and mending her dressing gown—all with great physical sacrifice. The 4711 cologne was always at the ready, the only bottle on her bedside table other than her various medications, but all this went beyond basic pride of self. There was apparently a time when all she had was pride, as she was growing old, alone with few friends and no financial resources. The days in the small calendars she had saved in her closet went by for days on end without a notation: no visitors, no appointments, no remarks. Then she would note she'd washed and curled her hair. This kind of attention to mundane detail and obvious lack of contact with the outside world was not only sad, but far more mysterious than the legendary persona she had so carefully developed. The box of calendars, devoid of entries, tells much about Djuna Barnes. It dispels much of the mystery.

The many photographs, clippings, and magazines saved by Barnes do the same. She retained almost anything that mentioned her name, all appropriately underlined. The photographs were usually captioned, often signed DJUNA BARNES, with a date and sometimes a location. There was rarely any mention of the photographer.

She never bothered to organize any of this material; she simply kept it in boxes in no order. A clipping from 1925 might rest next to one of forty years later, with appropriate passages underlined in red or blue. Photographs of herself and friends, reproductions of ancient paintings loose and unsorted mixed with hundreds of postcards from her to her relatives and from friends.

All this was but the tip of the iceberg; the bulk of her papers and similar material, as I've mentioned, had been transferred to the McKeldin Library long before I entered the picture. This most private of persons saved everything on paper that related to her or that she had created, made notations on much of it, and, in the end, made certain it was placed in a public institution knowing full well that no matter what restrictions she might place on it, eventually all the secrets she had hidden for so long would become known. This may appear peculiar on the face of it, but given the duality in Barnes, it makes a certain amount of sense.

She told me hundreds of times the only reason anyone does anything is for money, and it's clear this was the only reason she sold her papers to the University of Maryland, an institution she did not hold in particularly high regard. She wanted her papers at a more prestigious institution, but none evidenced any interest when they were for sale. The University of Maryland was willing to pay a decent sum. Barnes felt most of what she sold would be safe from too many prying eyes during her lifetime, and she desperately needed the money. One man on the staff of the McKeldin Library, Dr. Robert Beare, seemed sincere in his interest in her work. While she was upset that her papers had to be sold, that possibly someone she didn't respect might be able to look at them, she was pleased to have the papers cared for in some fashion, and, because of the covenants placed on their use, perhaps felt this might add to her aura.

She wanted me to burn everything that remained when she died, but eventually she arranged things so this couldn't happen. She wanted to burn them herself but was unable to do so. Now, everything is at the McKeldin Library. There were certain things she didn't want anyone to know, drafts she didn't want anyone to see, notebooks of ideas that were hers alone, but in the end she made certain all this material would fall into public hands. She coveted her secrets and lived a mysterious life, but she made certain all the secrets were written down and preserved or revealed over and over in conversations with me. This is pride beyond the curling iron, and this action indicated a most complex and thoroughly confused personality. We never discussed why she kept everything she had ever written; the only statement she ever made that related to all these papers was that there were a few good lines buried among the millions of words. I never brought it up and Barnes was not inclined to mention it herself.

If it was indelicate to discuss hoarding every scrap of paper, there was no problem when it came to discussing a wide range of other topics, including suicide and religion. She believed in the former but was suspicious of the latter. She said she'd often contemplated suicide and, with a wave of her hand in the direction of her bottles of medicine, said she knew she had everything necessary to kill herself. It was just a matter of summoning sufficient courage to do it and then to "do it beautifully." She told me she didn't have the courage to take her own life and had long passed the point where she could do it beautifully.

Religion was another matter. She was not consciously religious in a practicing way, but the topic fascinated her. She was fond of repeating the idea that the only thing she believed in was her own ignorance, that she was incapable of contemplating the existence of a supreme being. This was, of course, an easy out, one that has been taken by many, but it is obvious that much of her final work was distinctly religious in tone. It was on her mind and she liked to talk and write about it. Her conversation and her written words were not specific, but both were oriented towards Christianity. She never voiced any interest in other forms of religion but was mildly anti-semitic in conversation: one of her favorite catch-phrases was "How odd of God to choose the Jews." She never claimed the line to be original but used it as though she owned it.

There were hundreds of other topics: why Crown lavender smelling salts were the very best (a bottle was always near by); her years of great poverty (yes, she had spent the night on park benches in the past); her love of words and how they work together was more important than anything in the world, even as a child; the childhood doll still hidden away in a drawer; Guido Bruno's bad breath; the friend who took care of her pet canary and tried to replace it with a new one when the original died, but Barnes spotted the difference immediately; why toilet seats had to be wooden; the difference between "slap" and "strike" in "Quarry"; why all people with facial hair were hideous; why she couldn't accept Christmas gifts; the wonders of Chinese carry-out food (once she became brave enough to try it); hatred of the Academy of Arts and Letters ("I'm not in the select part because I'll not lick anyone's foot!"); how a well-meaning but foolish man ruined her painting "Alice," and even if it was restored perfectly it was no longer a work of hers but that of someone else; why she never voted; endless episodes concerning the radio commentary of Pegeen Fitzgerald and her "dreadful husband"; Dilly the cat and how it used to sit on her typewriter; climbing a ladder to reach a sleeping loft in her home as a child; Pearl, the drunken super who insisted on a five-dollar bribe or she'd paint her door black and never send the plumber; why the poor pour their hearts out to illusion; the story of returning Franz Joseph Haydn's skull to Vienna; how she loved a particularly glorious Swedish tenor, who's name she was unable to remember, a man who was even finer than Alfred Deller, and both these men were far superior to Frank Sinatra, but she liked Sinatra all the same and couldn't understand why; someone, probably the nurse, was stealing the tiny silver spoons without which her ginger ale and coffee ice cream would never be the same, so she kept one right next to her on the table full of medicine; how she was allergic to "all the deadly nightshades" but would eat them anyway, even if they were likely to shorten her life; Simple Simon; dinners with Dag Hammarskjold; that love and companionship were the most important things a person can have ("Make certain you have someone to grow old with, especially if they love you a great deal for even if you don't love them as much, it is foolish to give up the security of one who cares for you"); what did my parents look like, how did they treat me, could she please see a photograph ("My, how normal and in love they look"); and countless conversations dealing with the human condition ("Everyone is a rotten bastard. I don't trust anyone, even myself. When you can say that about yourself, you know its true"). That is how the year went by: much talk, organizing business affairs, and virtually no work on her part other than occasional publication of books overseas. As the year ended, however, it was clear all was not well. Barnes became considerably more forgetful and, in the process, more stubborn and quarrelsome. It was not a good omen.

New York,
1909

Nineteen eighty-one was the year of marked change in Barnes; less than six months into it we ceased working together. As her health slowly worsened she became increasingly insecure and complex. The decline in her health was accompanied by increasing lapses in her ability to comprehend simple matters. While I was certain that some of this inability was simply for show or her own amusement, it was difficult to discern whether she was being recalcitrant, or simply couldn't deal with a situation. She would also begin to say something, request a favor or agree to a contract, and then forget about it—but because of her pride and sensitivity, could never admit to forgetting. She was, in her mind, never incorrect. Just as she played games with her comprehension, forgetfulness was also used for her own purposes. Was it a total lapse of recall or was it an act? I was never sure. Our working relationship was becoming considerably more difficult.

Barnes's worsening physical condition was not noticeable on a day-to-day basis; her health was so poor that all one could perceive was longer coughing fits and diminishing energy. Her mental changes, which had begun in mid-to-late 1980, became considerably more disparate by early 1981. I was, regrettably, fascinated with the changes at first. I'd never witnessed anything like it. It was sad and frustrating because slowly, often imperceptively, someone I thought I knew very well was slowly changing into someone else. The person with the same name and social security number, it seemed, was now often another person, who frequently made no sense and frequently blamed her confusion on me.

Yet when she was lucid, in control of herself, relatively free of pain, and had not taken too many Darvon capsules or two sleeping pills the night before, she could summon up energy and want to work. It remained her greatest desire, to be pain free with sufficient energy to write. This passion to complete some work, any work, led to one of our strangest encounters.

One morning in late January 1981, Barnes called in a panic and asked if I'd come by and talk, just to settle her nerves. I found her to be extremely agitated; she'd suffered all night, spending the entire time "crawling up the wall," wracked with pain, anxiety, and depression. When I arrived she was so utterly frustrated she seemed on the verge of tears; I'd never seen her so distraught. Her first question was whether I knew of anything she could take to relieve her pain, which by now she believed was the result of cancer of the rectum. She was willing to take any medication, try anything. Nothing the doctors had given her afforded even a slight lessening of her constant agony. She said, "I want a few painless months to work and a little energy, and I don't care how I get it."

She was eighty-eight, aching, frustrated; her request perfectly reasonable given the circumstances of her unhappy existence. I told her there was probably a way, but it couldn't be done strictly legally, and in the end she'd wind up addicted to various opiates and other chemicals as well. There was even a good possibility the drugs might kill her, but the pain could be stopped. There was a sparkle in her eye as she said, "I've seen death before and I didn't like it, but I'd give up everything for six months of work." I told her this was a very risky course and she'd better consider all the possibilities and ultimate consequences. I also made up my mind to discuss the request with her doctor; I wasn't about to become involved in such a scheme without medical advice and appear as Mephistopheles dragging a Faustian Barnes into the depths of drug addiction. In reality, there was no need for concern; Barnes occasionally brought up the idea when she'd become sufficiently frustrated, but never made anything I interpreted as a serious request to proceed. So it became a non-issue. I don't know how seriously she considered the idea. As her mental facilities weakened she probably thought of such things less and less; at least she ceased to verbalize any strong interest in obtaining addictive drugs and probably remained content with the knowledge that the possibility existed.

Death was constantly on her mind. At eighty-eight, she was annoyed she had lived so long, but as she neared ninety decided it might be nice to somehow make it past her birthday. "I want to say I made ninety" was the way she put it and in the same breath usually added, "half that much would have been plenty; people should die at forty or forty-five, that's enough for anyone." I was forty when she said that to me, and I suggested that that many years were not quite enough. She then lectured me about growing old, how I probably never thought it would happen to me, but it would and I'd hate it just as she did at eighty-eight. I thought to myself that Barnes moved into her room on Patchin Place when she was my age and her life slowly came to a halt; she then began to experience time crawling by, her life becoming, to her, interminably long and unfulfilling. She often told me it was her feeling that as she aged time didn't go faster and faster, as everyone had told her would be the case; it went slower and slower. It went so slowly Barnes felt she had all the time she needed to finish her writing projects or to accomplish anything else she wished; she simply lacked the physical resources to utilize her time in a satisfactory fashion.

A week or two later, after a series of thoroughly pessimistic meetings, Barnes happened to be in a good mood. She looked at me and said, slightly mischeviously, "What if this isn't all there is? What if there's a hereafter? What if I die, then wake up and I'm sitting on a cloud?" Her attitude changed as she added, "What if I have to put up with this misery forever?" She laughed sarcastically, perhaps she was thinking of sitting on a cloud, still arguing with a clerk at Jefferson Market. Another day she said, "I'm beginning to remember things that happened to me before I was born. I know this isn't possible, but it's happening." These were feelings I wish

Barnes had developed with me in conversation, but she didn't. Perhaps they were just feelings, and she was never clear in her own mind about them, but I did notice she began to speak of her childhood much more frequently and often repeated the story of Colette remembering the names of everyone in one of her grade school classes a few days before she died. The excursions into Barnes's childhood were often interesting but, unfortunately, when she'd snap out of a temporary reverie, the present was still unpleasant.

Almost everything was wrong with Barnes's existence in this time: unrelenting pain, mental anguish, and never ending frustration. I suspect that as her memory and general mental ability diminished, it focused more and more of her attention on her physical difficulties. Everything in her life was a problem and as time passed I came to recognize I had become the major problem—at least so it seemed to Barnes—and part of it was my own fault.

Barnes had become increasingly dependent on me and hated this with a vengeance. Her dual nature raised its head, or by this time it perhaps would be proper to say her various natures raised their heads, and I could never be absolutely certain whom I was dealing with at any given moment. I knew she hated this dependence on me, but she was unwilling, unable in fact, to do almost anything for herself. Unfortunately for all concerned, she didn't trust anyone else to do what was required for her own existence or even the most trivial business matters. The problem was compounded by the circumstances; my activity on her behalf had to increase as her capacity diminished, and as she became more forgetful and infirm it became necessary to make more decisions to handle her affairs properly. Andrew Field, in his biography about her, suggested that I "presumed to exercise too much autonomy" with Barnes's affairs. He's partially correct, but I did not presume anything. I simply did what needed to be done, as efficiently and competently as possible. When Barnes was less able to participate in everything, I simply continued doing the job and, of course, this annoyed her. No amount of explanation on my part made any difference.

It was, naturally, a vicious circle, with no hope for a solution. The less Barnes was able to do or understand, the more was required of me. The more I did, with or without her participation, the less she understood and more frustrated she became— frustrated with herself for being infirm and with me for doing what she was unable to do on her own. Yet I was in place and better than a nurse because I didn't have to be with her all the time. She failed to comprehend, or didn't want to comprehend, that she not only needed me but required a full time nurse as well. She didn't want a nurse, but became increasingly annoyed with me for doing all the things she'd initially asked me to handle; her solution was to ask me more and more frequently, almost repeatedly, to assume the duties of a nurse and be with her part time on a daily basis. This was, of course, impossible and I'm certain she knew it but didn't want to face the reality of the situation, or was incapable of facing it, whether she wanted to or not.

I had just formed a new record company in January 1981 and was in the process of structuring a public offering of it in the summer. To fill up my plate I had closed my recording studio and was beginning to prepare a new residence on the other side of Green-wich Village at Broadway and 12th Street. I struggled to make time to attend to significant matters on Barnes's behalf, but I did not have the time, energy, or inclination to go to the grocery store everyday, cook meals, or perform the duties of a nurse, all of which Barnes began to expect as her condition worsened. No matters of significance were overlooked, but unfortunately for me a can of tomatoes at just the right time from the market had become far more important than the conclusion of a contract.

Barnes had lived alone in Patchin Place for over forty years and the idea of another person, a black stranger no less, in her room all the time was simply intolerable. I didn't blame her for this; it would have annoyed me as well, but Barnes would have been annoyed if she'd lived alone in a nine-room apartment. She just didn't want anyone around full time, regardless of the need, and, to rationalize her refusal, claimed she couldn't afford to hire one on a permanent basis. Maybe she believed this was true; she'd been on the edge of poverty for so long, often living off the largesse of friends, that there was every possibility she didn't understand she had a modest reserve of money in the bank. At the time she had about $180,000 on hand, a sum that if managed properly could have easily kept her in nurses for a number of years. Barnes's reality was that she didn't want a nurse and didn't want to spend the money. She wanted me to handle the job. My reality was I couldn't be with her as often as she required and wouldn't have been even if I had the time.

The result was frustration and annoyance at me for not doing her bidding. It was bad enough that I was assuming more and more responsibility: it was intolerable that I wouldn't do as I was told. Everything was failing. The typewriter wouldn't even work; she felt a new one might help her, but it had to be exactly like the model Peggy Guggenheim had given her years before. "The type is getting so light. None of the pens work; the ink fades as soon as I write it." The new typewriter didn't help; the type was just as light as that produced by the old one. The Divilbus pump, a device she was required to use three or four times a day to control her asthma, became plugged and she didn't know how to fix it. It often didn't matter if it was operating or not; the small bottles of liquid I kept lined on the bookshelf next to her bed like tiny brown soldiers were constantly spilled and misplaced. She was unable to fill the bottles herself, each had to be filled carefully, drop by drop, and she was unable to see anything as small and transparent as a drop. To add to her difficulty, she couldn't remember whether she'd used the pump, or taken any of her pills, if she didn't write it down. I filled the bottles twenty at a time, but I couldn't tell whether she'd used the medication even if the bottles were empty; it might have just been spilled.

If someone brought her flowers she'd be polite, but once the donor was gone, rage would set in for she was left with the responsibility of caring for them. Duality again; she didn't have the heart to throw them out, but hated her benefactor for adding to her misery because she now had to fill a vase with water. She claimed she didn't have the strength, that her life had been reduced to simply carrying water from the bathroom to the vase on her desk. She also had to fill the humidifier twice daily; it ran twenty-four hours a day when it was not burned out for lack of water, and if she had to do that, why should she have to water flowers as well? This was honestly one of Barnes's more serious concerns during this period: rage at flowers and filling a vase.

The roaches that ran races up the kitchen wall and danced at night under her bed also pointed to the failure of everything. Nothing worked on these creatures since Barnes's weak lungs made it impossible to spray anything that even had a remote possibility of being effective. The only possibility was a product called Hargate, some sort of natural spray that had no chemicals in it. Of course, it was about as effective as swearing at the roaches in the middle of the night. More creatures were disposed of by accidental drowning when the toilet flushed spontaneously than were ever eliminated by this seemingly useless aerosol.

I was amazed she tolerated all these annoyances as well as she did. She was reduced to taking pills that did no good, eating food she didn't like, and filling a humidifier that regularly burned out; I was increasingly "impertinent"; and she was being "tortured by everyone." One day, convinced she was being persecuted, she referred to hang-up telephone calls. "They're checking to see if I'm still alive." The next day no one had called; now people were avoiding her. Barnes had isolated herself for the second half of her life, but one day in her eighty-ninth year she looked at me and said how badly it felt to be cut off from everyone. No one ever wrote and few ever telephoned. One day she said, "I'll never call anyone ever again!" but she did and it was usually me.

One night in March she telephoned around midnight in a state of panic because the electric power had failed; there were no lights, radio, or even a breathing pump if she needed it in an emergency. If the cause was only a blown fuse she, couldn't understand the problem or see well enough to solve it. She was in despair. I drove in from New Jersey, wondering what would ever become of this legendary woman. She wasn't like the beauty queen whom no one asked for a date because it was assumed she was already engaged—but a woman who had isolated herself by choice. Had anyone tried to be of assistance they'd have been rejected.

When I arrived and let myself in, I found no power failure. One cord had come out of a wall socket. The tangle of wires linking an electric blanket, clock, radio, lamps, pump, television, and other items was confusing for someone who could see. The frustration of witnessing the simple solution to the problem merely added to her despair for she saw herself as not only utterly dependent on me (or anyone) for various circumstances outside her control, but she appeared incompetent as well. She was helpless and knew it. Shame made the situation even worse, and she was clearly worried that this sad state of affairs might reach ears outside her room. She didn't want the world to know the indomitable Miss Barnes had indeed been dominated by time.

Shortly after this late-evening episode came the final insult, the final failure. Barnes telephoned me at my office one afternoon and asked that I please come by as soon as it was convenient. It was not a life or death situation she said, but would I please hurry. I arrived a short while later and found her sitting on the edge of her bed, disheveled, with almost no color in her face. She looked helpless. Most of the bottles on the table beside her bed were overturned or on the floor. Next to her, on the bed, was a crumpled paper bag. She looked at me and said, "They always told me I could do it with what I had at hand and I tried, but it didn't work."

She'd taken all her bottles of medicine and emptied them into the paper bag, taken two handfuls of the pills, and swallowed them with a few gulps of ginger ale. The result was nothing more than an upset stomach; the pills didn't even make her drowsy. She had summoned the courage to try to kill herself, but it didn't work: she'd failed. Time and time again she told me about her stay in the hospital, when the orderly had told her she could kill herself with a massive dose of the medication at hand. Now she knew it wasn't so and found herself left with nausea, a paper bag full of pills, and even more despair.

She asked if I would please sort the pills and return them to their proper bottles. She would continue to take her medication as prescribed and push on towards ninety. I gathered up the bottles from the table and the floor and took them to her desk. The first thing I noticed was that in her hurry she'd failed to empty two or three of the bottles into the bag; one that was still intact contained the sleeping pills. I said nothing.

Her nausea passed and she became hungry. She asked that I order something for both of us from Hunan Royal, the closest Chinese carryout. I agreed and as I was walking out the door to go pick it up, she reminded me to make absolutely certain no soy sauce was used in the preparation of her dish, that the doctor had said she should avoid salt. I shook my head in wonder as I walked up to Twelfth Street; I arrived and the owner asked, "How's grandma?" He had been making special lo mein dishes for me for over a year. By habit I said she was just fine and then added "watch the soy sauce." How silly it was, I thought, Barnes had just tried to kill herself, the ultimate act of trying to deprive oneself of life itself, and when this proved to be impossible, the next best thing was to deprive herself of a tasty meal, because the salt in the soy sauce was against her doctor's orders.

It was easy to understand her anger toward me and I saw it building day by day, particularly as I became increasingly unavailable for mundane chores. She had reached a stage when her own sense of worth was so damaged she had to strike back at any object of her anger and make every effort to assert herself in every way possible. One form of this became almost constant criticism of virtually everything I did; if I'd managed to walk on water, I'm certain at this stage she'd wonder why I hadn't been able to run on it as well.

Now, everytime we met, she'd find something to argue about; if there wasn't something new it was always possible to tell me how I'd ruined her reputation with my brief four-paragraph foreword in *Ryder* (see Appendix II). She'd complained about this constantly for the past year (she never did when it was issued), and for the most part I'd just ignored her comments and failed to respond to anything. One day, however, she complained one time too often and, much to her surprise, I suggested that if her reputation was so fragile it could be ruined by my totally acceptable foreword—which she'd approved—then her reputation was very shaky indeed, and no purpose could be served by her constant complaining about it. I reminded her that I'd made certain the offending foreword was removed, by contract, in all proposed foreign editions, but nothing could excise it from the eight thousand or so copies circulating in the United States. This shocked her into silence, at least temporarily, but it was clear she was trying everything she could to provoke me. She tried in other ways, one of the most amusing having to do with tending to her various bank accounts.

Barnes had deposits at four local savings banks. The amount at each was fairly substantial and I had the funds in high interest certificates of deposit. It would have been possible to obtain even better rates, but she was unwilling to tie her funds up for a period longer than six months. She understood nothing of the banking system or even how banks worked in 1981. Since the accounts were short term I renewed each twice a year; if I hadn't, the funds would have reverted to low interest, ordinary savings accounts, the conditions in which I had found them in 1978.

I always tried to find the best rate, a quarter of point here or there. At the time all the savings banks were highly competitive, vying for every possible depositor by offering various incentives, usually household appliances. In early 1981 the bonuses for a deposit of forty to fifty thousand dollars became substantial and, mistakenly, I took a list of every bonus available to Barnes and suggested she pick something out. One of the banks was offering a color television set for a deposit; in fact her money was already in that bank and all she had to do was renew her certificate. I told her it might be nice to have a small color set. It could rest close to her bed and replace the dreadful vintage-1960 black and white monstrosity on the other side of the room.

She was horrified when she learned of the bank's program. How dare they give away "prizes"! How dare they try to lure customers away from other banks with promises of free gifts! She wouldn't have any of it and didn't want her money in any bank that engaged in such underhanded tactics. She wanted her money in honorable banks that did not give away toasters. She didn't believe me when I explained that all the banks did it, that it would be almost impossible to find any savings bank in the city not offering free goods. Barnes, however, felt that as a matter of principle, banks should not engage in such "un-bank-like" activities. She didn't want a television, she didn't want anything, and she didn't want me to accept anything either. If I wanted a television for myself she'd buy me one, but her principles required she accept nothing from the bank. We argued about this until the day the certificate had to be renewed, but she wouldn't budge. She didn't care even if she could give the "gifts" to anyone of her choosing: the entire situation was simply immoral. She was infuriated with banks, bankers, and their methods; there was nothing lower than a banker in her mind, unless it was someone who pirated her work.

Circumstances like this became the norm; arguments over trivialities and her constant fear of the "snake pit," the nursing home to which she was certain she would be confined if her relatives had the chance. It didn't matter when I told her she was well-protected from that eventuality as matters stood, but as events were developing, matters were standing on crumbling foundations.

In late May I had to go away for nearly a week on recording business in Nashville. I'd provided Barnes with a list of emergency numbers; there was still a number of young ladies who were always ready, eager to meet the legendary lady of Patchin Place.

Things went well in Nashville; I telephoned once or twice to make certain she was all right. There seemed to be no problems and towards the end of my stay I found a copy of Allen Tate's only novel, *The Fathers*, a book Barnes had said she'd like to see again. I returned to New York on 24 May and after unpacking my bags headed over to see her, with the Tate book in hand.

I arrived to find her in a frenzy; where had I been, how dare I stay away so long. It couldn't go on this way any longer: I had to give up my control over her. She kept repeating, "You had control over me and I can't stand it!" She said she no longer wanted me to look after her affairs, she no longer wanted me to be her literary executor, she'd found others to do the job. She was preparing a new will and removing me as executor of the estate, but was "remembering" me nonetheless, for all the work I'd done in her behalf. She wanted to continue seeing me, but in no "official" capacity.

Barnes blurted all this out very quickly. She was terrified when she said it, almost like a well-rehearsed speech; and when she stopped talking she appeared to brace herself for a serious argument. To her surprise and perhaps frustration, I made no specific reply to her tirade other than to say if this was the way she wanted things, it was just fine with me. I added that it wouldn't take much effort for her new found assistants to maintain the literary side of her affairs; all the important work to insure the orderly publication of her work overseas was in place, and thus there was little for anyone to do for the foreseeable future. I took out the large chart listing all the books and pointed out the few loose ends remaining. The banking matters were also under control; the certificates of deposit had been recently renewed and had three to five months to run; the lowest level accountant could handle these matters easily.

My attitude only added to her frustration. She had taken what she perceived as a major step, which she'd probably worried over for weeks or perhaps months. That I reacted in the same way as if she'd inquired of the weather aggravated her condition even more. She began to vent her anger beyond the usual "you ruined my reputation" kind of nonsense. At one point she said I was the cause of "the death of Miss Barnes!" I thought this somewhat farfetched but still didn't contradict her or offer any rejoinder. I tried to make small talk for a few moments, mentioned the Allen Tate book, but she was far too excited and frustrated to be interested. I decided it was time to leave and as I put the book back in a tote-bag noticed there were a few chocolate morsels in the large jar on the mantel. Barnes knew I liked chocolate, and the jar was kept full, courtesy of the Jefferson Market. It had been almost empty for some while, a good indication of the increasing strain in our working relationship. I stood up, walked over to the jar, emptied the dozen or so remaining morsels into my hand, and said I had to be going. Barnes had a look of amazement on her face and said, "I'm totally disoriented, nothing makes any sense." I replied it certainly didn't, wished her good afternoon, and left. Her parting words were, "Goodbye Mr. O'Neal."

I never went back but did have a few telephone conversations with her during the next few months. There was no point in returning; it was clear that my simple presence was an aggravation to her. I wasn't certain then why this was the case, but it was undoubtedly true, and I had no wish to add to her torment. That I was extremely busy with my own affairs and recognized that Barnes's literary and financial affairs were in good order, at least for the time being, made my decision easier. I had done what I could for her, and knew I could never provide what she now expected and required. She needed a full-time nurse and an accountant for an hour a week merely to maintain the status quo as her life ebbed away.

I walked away with no animosity; she had told me she didn't trust herself, but the woman in 1981 was not the same Djuna Barnes with whom I'd had a lively relationship. My experience with her had been very interesting and rewarding; this made up for the times when it was so unsettling. I'd learned a great deal from her and about her, discovered the secrets and mysteries of the mighty and impenetrable Djuna Barnes, but had no interest in discovering anything about the Barnes of 1981, a wholly different person. It would require far too much effort to unravel her new personality. There wouldn't be time to do it anyway, for she would just continue to change as the days went by. She had often told me "the real Djuna Barnes is dead." This may or may not have been the case in 1978, but it certainly was in May 1981, at least as far as I was concerned.

I also had no interest in watching her deteriorate, becoming weaker and more irrational. Barnes had been a fascinating person most of the time we worked together, and I wanted to remember that; if I continued to see her, matters could only become worse. I telephoned her about three weeks after our final meeting in May. She was astounded that I had simply dropped out of her life; she added that just because she wanted to change things didn't mean she never wanted to see me again. I lamely suggested that it was perhaps best to let the dust settle and then we might have some nice conversations once more. She was very conciliatory and agreed with what I said, but by the end of the conversations the old demons began to creep back in: "you know, you did ruin my reputation," and so forth. Despite a few additional telephone calls, this was our last proper conversation. She died a year later, a few days after her ninetieth birthday. She reached that milestone, as she had wished, but also found herself, at least temporarily, in a nursing home, courtesy of her relatives. She had always felt that would be the case and, if I can rely on the commentary of friends who saw her during her final months, found her last days like so many that had gone before, painful and nasty.

The mystery of Djuna Barnes, if there ever was one, was stripped bare. Nothing made any difference in the end as she raged helplessly against the results of her own creation. She'd created an aura about herself, made herself mysterious, and lived a secluded life to protect her creation, but there came a time when her system didn't work any longer and it began to crash in about her. Like a star burning out, once the process of collapse toward a black hole begins, it is irreversible. She had created her own world with her own values: she was the centerpiece, but the system was flawed and once it began to disintegrate, she was unable to stop the process as it slowly reached its inevitable conclusion. I returned to New York City from Maine a few days after her death, found an old *New York Times*, and read the obituary. Later in the day I walked next door to the Strand Bookstore to see what might have come in while I was away. There was a new title on the remainder table: *Selected Works of Djuna Barnes*. I already had a copy.

EPILOGUE:
A TELEPHONE
CALL FROM
THE PAST

New York,
turn-of-the-century

*I*n early 1986, just as I was beginning to put the finishing touches on this modest memoir of the time I spent with Djuna Barnes, there was a bizarre occurrence I am still unable to explain.

I've been involved in the music business for over twenty years. In the last ten I've handled thousands of cassettes that have come to my office: demonstrations by aspiring artists, samples of various masters, and other items. Many of these tapes were returned to the sender, providing postage had been enclosed or if they called for them, but as often as not they tended to pile up in boxes over the years and were reused for one purpose or another. One busy day in January I needed a cassette to make a copy, and instead of my going to the supply room to search out a discarded cassette or a blank, I hurriedly looked about my desk hoping to find a suitable candidate for the duplicator. I saw a Maxell C-60 with no identification that looked as though it would do just fine since I carefully label everything I wish to retain. I placed the cassette in the duplicator but for some reason, I don't know why, I decided to check it and see if anything was recorded on it.

I turned on the machine; there was no sound. Good, I thought, a blank. I pushed the rewind button to return the tape to the beginning but was surprised when it took so long to rewind completely. It finally reached the head and then, again for no explicable reason, I decided to see if anything was recorded near the beginning. I pushed the play button: to my surprise I heard a ringing telephone. I was puzzled for I could not recall ever having recorded a telephone conversation. The ringing ceased and Djuna Barnes answered the telephone.

I was dumbstruck. I listened to the conversation; judging from the topic it must have been recorded in 1979 or 1980. But I never consciously recorded Barnes. Could this, I thought, have been accidentally recorded on my telephone answering machine? If so, how did it get out of the machine and survive for so many years? More importantly, how did it get on my desk that particular day? My desk has been cleared off nearly two thousand times since 1979–80; in fact it has moved from one location to another and I've gone through at least three answering machines. How did this tape find its way to my desk and what possessed me to play it rather than merely pushing the high-speed duplicating button, as I normally do when I want to make a copy? None of it made any sense, then or now, but I quickly took the cassette out of the machine and removed the two tabs from the cassette that prevent accidental erasure. I labeled it properly and filed it away. This was, after all, a tangible, audible souvenir of my days with Djuna Barnes.

Everything is on this short cassette: Barnes is, as usual, proper to a fault, her basic consideration for others is evident: her memory fails and she then resorts to mental gymnastics when the failure becomes evident to her, and finally there is the anger at the doctor for being away for the weekend. It brought back many memories. The short conversation we had that day was as follows:

BARNES: Hello, Hello.

O'NEAL: Miss Barnes?

BARNES: Yes.

O'NEAL: It's Hank O'Neal.

BARNES: Yes.

O'NEAL: I'm sorry I didn't get to you earlier. I got stuck in the tunnel; it was great. I thought I should tell you I wasn't able to convince the doctor, Dr. Beck's substitute, to give you sleeping pills, because he doesn't know you.

BARNES: No, he doesn't know anything about me but it isn't necessary. I'll call him.

O'NEAL: But Dr. Beck isn't there. He won't be in until Monday.

BARNES: It's O.K. I've got plenty and I don't take them often. I can't recall ever taking them except once.

O'NEAL: But you said you needed them, that you weren't able to sleep.

BARNES: I didn't say that at all, but I don't want to contradict you. I'm tired of arguing, so I didn't say anything. Let's just forget it. I really don't need them now. When I need them I can call him back; he'll be back someday I suppose. He'll be back Monday. That's plenty of time.

O'NEAL: O.K.

BARNES: Thank you just the same.

O'NEAL: All right, I'll get the bank things done tomorrow and I'll let you know how it goes.

BARNES: Would this be for *Ryder*?

O'NEAL: Yes, this is for *Ryder*. I'll be going to the bank tomorrow afternoon.

BARNES: I don't understand the whole thing but never mind. You just go ahead.

O'NEAL: O.K., I'll bring you your copy because you must keep one copy of it.

BARNES: Yes.

O'NEAL: O.K.

BARNES: O.K. Thank you.

O'NEAL: All right, goodnight.

BARNES: I probably owe you something.

O'NEAL: Not at all. Nothing.

BARNES: Thank you.

O'NEAL: Goodnight.

BARNES: Goodnight.

APPENDIX I:
UNPUBLISHED
BERENICE ABBOTT
PHOTOGRAPHS

*I*n the early 1950s Berenice Abbott photographed Djuna Barnes. The eighteen portraits were made in Abbott's studio at 50 Commerce Street in New York City. Barnes referred to this photographic encounter on numerous occasions (p. 119), but her memory of the event was distinctly different from what is revealed by the photographic evidence. It is perfectly apparent that Abbott did not trick her; she is shown coming through the door three times.

The negatives for these portraits are still in very good condition, perhaps because they have rarely been printed. Only one, #10, has ever been published; this image was used in a cropped version as a cover illustration for Louis F. Kannenstine's 1977 critical study, *The Art of Djuna Barnes—Duality and Damnation* (New York University Press). An uncropped version serves as a frontispiece for the book. These negatives are very dense and require care in printing. Image #3 was taken without extra lighting, #10 is slightly out of focus, and #18 is very thin (and torn at the bottom), probably because Abbott exposed it hurriedly just as Barnes was preparing to leave.

It is likely these photographs are the most accurate record of how Barnes appeared during this period of her life. I know of no other series of photographs of her after she returned from Europe and went into seclusion. There may have been others, but I have only seen two other sittings where multiple images resulted: Abbott's (the cover image and that on p. 103) and the Van Vechten portrait (on p. 71, which is one of at least eight). The negatives for these photographs by Berenice Abbott are owned and maintained by Commerce Graphics Ltd. Inc., 160 East Union Avenue, East Rutherford, New Jersey 07073. Permission to use them may be obtained by contacting this company.

APPENDIX II: FOREWORD

This is the "offending" foreword I wrote for the
1979 reissue of Ryder. *It only appears in the*
U.S. edition published by St. Martin's Press,
now out of print.

*R*yder, Djuna Barnes's first published extended work, was originally issued in August 1928 in a small edition of three thousand copies. The book is slightly autobiographical in nature, at least to the extent that various characters in the narrative are easily traced to Miss Barnes's immediate family (including herself as a minor character) and circle of friends.

Initial critical reaction to *Ryder* was mixed and ranged from "the most amazing book ever written by a woman" in the *Saturday Review* to outright hostility in other publications. Almost all critical readers, however, were befuddled by the complexity of the book as they were at the same time awed by the technical virtuosity of the language and the attempt to blend prose, poetry, a one-act play, and illustrations.

The opinions of the critics mattered little to the book-buying public; the somewhat Rabelaisian nature of *Ryder* insured brisk sales and for a short while it was ranked on various bestseller lists in the autumn of 1928. This public reaction caught the original publisher, Horace Liveright, unaware and the first edition was quickly sold out. The type had already been struck when it was realized the book was a modest success and by the time it could be reset and the second edition appeared, the demand had waned. The second edition remained in print for a few years and then vanished. There were occasional requests for the book for nearly fifty years, but a dispute between Miss Barnes and the publisher prevented a new edition. The copyright is now in Miss Barnes's name, thus this reissue.

This new issue of *Ryder* is nearly a facsimile of the 1928 edition. Miss Barnes has chosen to delete her original foreword, which dealt with censorship in the United States, but has elected not to restore the censored passages, which are indicated with asterisks throughout the text. Nine drawings illustrated the first edition and have been retained here. Two additional drawings, created by her for the first edition but not used at the time, have been added. These drawings head Chapters 12 and 15. The inspiration for all these drawings, as well as many other illustrations by Miss Barnes, was *L'Imagerie Populaire*, an anthol-

"IN MY CASE IT HAS ONLY BEEN PAINFUL AND NASTY."

ogy of illustrations compiled and published in Paris by Pierre
Louis Ducharte and Rene Saulnier in 1926: she freely and grate-
fully acknowledges her debt to this publication.

Hank O'Neal

APPENDIX III:
QUOTATIONS
FROM THE
JOURNAL OF
MARIE
BASHKIRTSEFF

*I*t is abundantly clear that most of the ideas that shaped the Djuna Barnes I knew in the years 1978–81 had been formulated early in her life. Much has been made about her family situation; indeed, Barnes made much of it herself, but even though all the circumstances in her writing from *Ryder* through *The Antiphon* are undoubtedly significant in her development, I suspect there is a good deal more to Barnes than just a wicked father and other assorted relatives and rascals.

There are clues to the influences on Barnes in the books she read in her formative years. This became particularly clear after I removed about fifteen cartons of books from her oversized closet to make room for a nurse. The books were stored at my studio, and I often browsed through the boxes. The most revealing I came upon was entitled the *Journal of Marie Bashkirtseff*. The book was dusty, yellowing, and in poor condition; it had probably been unopened for years. I had never heard of it and still know nothing of the reputation it may have once enjoyed; I suspect it may have had some sort of following many years ago. In 1980 it seemed very foolish, to say the least, but in the mid-teens this book made what seems to have been a remarkable impression on Djuna Barnes.

It is important to understand that Barnes was generally very careful with her books, not so much in physical terms but with regard to ownership. She usually wrote her name in her books. If a book had been acquired second-hand, she went so far as to indicate that underlined portions were not done by herself. On occasion she also indicated pages on which she'd made notations. It was as though she knew someone would be looking at her books after her death. The Bashkirtseff journal is, however, unique among the books of Barnes that I observed. It is not only extensively underlined but is annotated in some instances in such a way as to indicate that certain passages refer to Barnes herself, and it also includes a drawing.

The book was written in the late nineteenth century; Barnes's copy was dated 1913. The handwriting in the book and the drawing seem to come from about the same time. She had underlined many passages; some of the more interesting follow:

"I find more charm in old satins, tarnished gildings, antique pillars and ornaments, than in trimmings, rich, gaudy and flaring. p. 32

"I being, as usual, the life of the party. p. 34

"He was as light to my soul, and that light has gone out. It is dark, dreary, sad. I know not which way to turn. Before this, in my slight annoyances, I could always find some ray of comfort, some light to guide and give me strength; but now, wherever I seek I look around and feel. I find nothing but darkness. It is terrible! terrible! when there is nothing in the depth of your soul. [Barnes has added here: 'passionately in love with the idea of love.'] p. 41

"I feel sorry for those poor unfortunates who, having no real sorrows, make martyrs of themselves for want of something to do. [Barnes has added, 'Me!'] p. 42

"I am like those unfortunate artists who conceive a picture above their capacity to execute. p. 42

"I am but a dreamer, without a future, and full of ambition. Such is my lot! such is my life! I had it planned in my thoughts. p. 43

"We should not be seen too often, not even by those who love us. We must keep ourselves at a distance, abandon regrets and illusions, by such means we will appear better. p. 43

"Say what you will, fine dresses count for much. p. 44

"If I could only hide myself far, far away! where no one could see me, perhaps then I could recover my peace of mind. p. 44

"Were I sarcastic, I would say misfortune and love are synonymous. I do not say so, for love is what is most beautiful in the world. I compare myself to water which is frozen in its depths, with the surface alone agitated, for nothing either interests or amuses me in my depths. p. 46

"I am burning with impatience to tell my fortune before a mirror. p. 46

"I can now understand how one may have a passion for churches and convents. p. 48

"If we think we love no one, it is a mistake. If the object of our affection is not a man, it is a dog or a piece of furniture, and we love as strongly, only in another way. Were I in love I should want to be loved as I love. I would suffer nothing, not even a word for someone else. Such love is not to be found, therefore I shall never love, for no one will ever love me as I can love. p. 49

"I shall be punished for my pride and stupid arrogance. p. 49

"You may follow me from cradle to grave; for the life of a person, an entire life without disguises or lies, is always a grand and interesting thing. p. 50

"Let us love dogs and dogs only. Men and cats are unworthy things. p. 50

"All happens for the best, we can not escape our destiny. [Barnes has circled this old Russian proverb.] p. 50

"What I love best, when there is no one worth being with, is solitude. p. 51

". . . it may be stupid to praise one's self so much, but writers always describe their heroines, and I am my own heroine. p. 51

"I resemble that painting. My own photograph can never do me justice, that incomparable whiteness, freshness and delicate coloring. p. 53

"It is only when I am happy and peaceful that I am lovely. When tired or angry I am not beautiful but rather ugly. p. 53

"I would like others to feel as I do; but it is impossible, they would have to be me. p. 55

"I find everything good and agreeable, even tears, even pain. I love to weep. I love to be in despair. I love to be sad and sorrowful. p. 55

"I have never yet harmed anyone, but I have already been offended, calumniated, humiliated. How can I love men? I detest them, but God will not permit me to hate. p. 56

"I do not hide my suffering under the mask of a cowardly hypocrisy, as the rogue Job, who, while mincing to our Lord, made Him his dupe. p. 56

"I do not know if I will be understood—because it pains me to see stains accumulated on a gown which should have been kept spotless. p. 56

"I bought a novel; I do not remember at which station. It was so badly written, that, fearing to spoil my style, which is already bad enough, I threw it out the window and returned to my Herodotus. p. 57

"Let me see, I must collect my ideas. The more I have to tell, the less I have to write. p. 59

"I adore painting, sculpture, art, wherever it may be found. I could spend entire days in these galleries. p. 59

"Ah, the world is degenerating, we feel like sinking into the earth. [At the bottom of this page, Barnes executed a pencil drawing of a nude figure, presumably a woman, and titled it 'Shame!?'] p. 61

"How good it is to speak of him! How pure is the recollection! In thinking of him, I leave Nice behind me, I elevate myself, I love. When I think of this I can not write much; I think, I love, and that is all. p. 63

"I despise men profoundly and from conviction. I expect nothing good of them. They have not what I seek and hope for—a good and perfect soul. Those who are good are stupid and those who are intelligent are schemers or too much occupied with their intellect to be good. Moreover, each creature is essentially selfish; seek for goodness in a selfish man, you will find interest, deceit, intrigue, envy! Happy are they who have ambition. It is a noble passion;

through vanity and ambition we strive to appear good before others, and, if only momentarily, it is better than never. p. 64

"The day will undoubtedly come when I shall think I have found a man, but on that day I shall be sadly mistaken. I well foresee the day I shall be blinded. p. 64

"I shall continue my cerebral romance. p. 66

"There are peaceful souls, there are beautiful deeds, and there are honest hearts; but they are so rarely met with that we must not confound them with the rest of the world. p. 66

"Nothing will be found for there is nothing. p. 66

"I believe I could not be prouder nor more haughty than I am. p. 66

"In my moments of thirst for greatness, all objects seem unworthy to be touched, my pen refuses to write a commonplace word. I look upon my surroundings with supernatural disdain and say to my-self, sighing: 'Come, courage, the present is but a passage leading to where all will be well.' [Barnes has added, 'I hope so.'] p. 67

"The more I say, the less I will be believed. p. 68

"Is it not a sin to do as I do? Some saints have made vows; yes, but I seem to make conditions. No, God sees that my intention is good, and if I do wrong He will forgive me, for I wish to do right. p. 70

"My God, pardon me and take pity on me; allow me to accomplish my promises. [Barnes has added, 'To myself & clients.'] p. 70

"If I do wrong, I do it unconsciously. Pardon! p. 70

" 'You know,' he said, 'I don't promise to wear this glove upon my heart, that would be silly; but it will serve as a pleasant souvenir.' p. 83

"I seek, I find, I invent a man, I live in him, I swear only by him. I mix him up in everything, and then, when he has completely taken possession of my fickle mind I become bored and perhaps sad and tearful. I am far from desiring that this should happen, and I only say it from an instinctive feeling that it will." p. 83

This was the final passage underlined by Barnes. On the two or three following pages two sentences have stars beside them but nothing else. It is unclear if she ever finished the book but it is apparent she managed to read seriously the first eighty-plus pages.

That this book is by present standards a foolish concoction of mystical, pseudo-philosophical nonsense is beyond dispute, but something in it was in concert with Barnes's feelings in the mid-teens. I saw hundreds of her books; no other was annotated in such a manner. That so many underlined passages relate directly to so much in her life, not just in the distant past but in 1982 as well, is fascinating. Read the passages and then recall how Barnes led her life and her professed beliefs.

It is possible to give lengthy explanations about events or ideas that relate to these quotations, pointing out how various aspects of Barnes's life coincide with Bashkirtseff's ramblings. Ideal love, solitude, mystery, martyrdom for ideals, inability to complete ambitious projects, ambivalent feelings towards men, a strong belief in one's own virtue: all these are present in the way Barnes felt and lived her life. How much she was influenced by the book, if at all, is another matter. Perhaps the young Barnes viewed these ideas as a simple affirmation of her own deeply held beliefs. We will never know, but no matter what the reason or influence, it is nonetheless an interesting bit of information about the Djuna Barnes of 1913–1915. It would have been interesting to see how she might have reacted to this book—and the passionately under-lined, starred, and annotated phrases—had she seen it at ninety.

APPENDIX IV:
THE PROPOSED
PARIS REVIEW
INTERVIEW

*I*n September 1980 George Plimpton telephoned and suggested we meet. He was interested in my trying to convince Barnes to consent to a *Paris Review* interview. I explained to Plimpton and his associates, Fayette Hickok and Hollie Gay Walden, it was highly unlikely that Barnes would consider an interview, even in the prestigious *Paris Review*. Except for an inconsequential piece in the *New York Times* in the 1960s, she'd been silent for years and had never consented to an interview of the type then featured in the *Paris Review*. Despite my negative feelings they urged that I at least make an effort to convince Barnes of the worthiness of their request.

Armed with a tote bag full of back issues, courtesy of Plimpton, I met with Barnes and told her of my meeting as casually as possible. Expecting a shriek of horror, I was surprised when she didn't reject the idea out of hand and, in fact, seemed initially fascinated by the idea. Her reaction, of course, was prefaced with the remark that she'd never consented to a serious interview, and there was probably no reason why she should break her self-imposed rules at this time of her life. But I could tell she was thinking about the proposal.

Sensing a breakthrough of sorts, I suggested it might be interesting to consider an "interview," one she could use as a forum if she wished, even carefully structuring the questions she wished to answer. She looked at me, smiled slyly, and probably said something like "you devil." Over the next few days we spoke casually of the possibility and then suddenly one afternoon Barnes suggested I write out some ideas that could be developed into good questions. We'd go over them the next day.

I began working on them immediately; I'd finish a few, give them to her to evaluate, she'd make suggestions, and then I'd rewrite them. After a few weeks twenty-four questions and/or topics were completed. Some were general, others very specific. She seemed pleased with what we'd done, but in late October she changed her mind, expressing dismay that she had even entertained the idea of an interview for a second, even one structured by herself. We never discussed the proposal after that final decision.

* * *

The questions that follow are the final version we prepared. There are, obviously, no answers, but because Barnes helped structure them and approved of the topics, they become answers in a way.

1. You claim you refuse to be interviewed about the craft of writing because it is impossible to tell anyone how to write and consequently you have nothing to say. While it is perhaps impossible to tell anyone how to write, your private conversation indicates you have a good deal to say about the craft and, in relating the how and why of your own experience in developing and evolving your own talents, don't you feel you might provide encouragement or inspiration to others?

2. Your first published work was poetry, but what was the form of your first serious attempts at writing? When did it occur to you that you were or wanted to be a writer?

3. As you were being educated by your family, were there any books or specific writers who influenced you? Do you still regard any of these early influences highly? Do you feel there are certain writers and/or books any serious writer should reread on a regular basis?

4. Personal morality seems to be a significant factor in your own writing. You once said you always felt that if you ever committed an immoral act or were dishonorable in any way, you would be unable to write a word. How has this concept guided your writing? Has it made a difference in what you have written and do you consciously incorporate this penchant for morality in your work?

5. Your very early work is much different from the later. In 1941 you said *Ulysses* had changed the aspirations of those who had hoped for a literary career overnight. How did your encounter with Joyce and his writings change yours? Is this why you reject almost all of the writing you did prior to meeting him? How did you go about adjusting to the ideas presented to you by Joyce?

6. You are concerned with the precise meaning of words, yet you often juxtapose archaic usage with extremely accurate contemporary meanings. What is your reason for this? Has the devaluation of language, the obvious alteration of word meaning over the years, seriously affected your writing? How have you coped with these changes?

7. What is the relationship between the way you use words and the ideas you want the words to convey. Which is paramount, the way you use the words or the story you wish to tell? Do you try to create new knowledge with your writing? Is this an obligation of a writer or is it sufficient simply to convey ideas in the abstract?

8. You keep notebooks in which you have stored good lines for future use, to incorporate in work at a later date. Have you always found this a useful way of working?

9. The autobiographical nature of your writing is more apparent in your later work. Is the subject matter of this writing a product of your memory that you do not understand, or do you understand it completely and use it as a creative springboard?

10. In both *Ryder* and *Ladies Almanack* you experimented with language and archaic styles of word usage. Is it important for a writer to experiment in this fashion?

11. In the late 1920s, following the publication of *Ryder* and *Ladies Almanack*, it appears you began consciously and carefully to craft your writing, culminating a few years later with *Nightwood*. Is this a valid observation and, if so, how did you alter your approach to writing in this period?

12. How did *Nightwood* evolve? Did you have an overall structure or concept before you began, or did it come in pieces and develop as you wrote it?

13. In the early 1930s Boni & Liveright rejected the first version of *Nightwood*. How did you change this rejected draft to become the final version as published by Faber & Faber in 1935? Have you ever relied on editors for any work you consider serious? You rewrite for your own purposes a great deal; have you ever rewritten anything for an editor?

14. In *Nightwood* your writing became not only more complex and multilayered but filled with such an abundance of ideas that misinterpretation became commonplace. Readers and critics alike have read many things into this book that distress you; are there any ambiguities you might care to clarify?

15. Upon the completion of *Nightwood* did you feel you had written as good a work of this type as was possible for you? Is this why you never wrote another novel?

16. Do critics play any part in the creative process? You are very fond of both T. S. Eliot and Edwin Muir and respect their critical ability, but did they or any others have any particular influence on you?

17. Appearing nearly twenty-five years after *Nightwood*, *The Antiphon* brings many of your characters full cycle. In it you have created a work with extraordinarily complex ideas and imagery, combined with what appears to be intentional ambiguity. What was your purpose in structuring the play in such a fashion?

18. The *Times Literary Supplement* said of *The Antiphon* ". . . the real reason for the use of the dramatic form is to create a formal complexity beyond the range of other verse forms and the complexity is integral to her vision. . . . and since all this is deliberate it is outside the scope of conventional criticism." Do you feel this is an accurate statement and if so, why did you wish to place yourself beyond the range of the critics with this play? Has this also been the case with much of your later extremely complex poetry?

19. To what extent should a writer use his craft to comment on the world around him? In *The Antiphon* were you commenting on the state of contemporary theater as well as the human condition and frailty of emotions?

20. The poetry you have written in recent years has, for the most part, been withheld from publication. You have elected to refine this newest work very carefully. How does the way you write today differ from the manner in which you wrote sev-

enty years ago? The meanings of words have changed; do you feel there have been equally dramatic changes in the human condition?

21. At a time when most poetry is devoid of craft, when anyone, regardless of talent, can call himself or herself a poet and usually get away with it, why are you silent? Do you feel a writer has any obligation other than silence?

22. You seem to think in a cyclical fashion, often in a most pessimistic way, i.e., your image of the pram and baby rolling towards an open grave. It also seems true of your work as well; you began as a poet and now in your old age are concentrating exclusively on poetry. How do you view your most recent work? Do you feel it is anything more than an extension of life's repetitious uselessness? If so, do such feelings affect your creative output at the age of eighty-eight?

23. Is the sincere questioning of one's own work a necessity of being a good writer? You seem to question your own finest work in a very serious manner.

24. Have you ever been completely satisfied with anything you've written?